LINCOLN'S NEW SALEM

LINCOLN'S
NEW SALEM

By BENJAMIN P. THOMAS

Drawings by ROMAINE PROCTOR

[NEW AND REVISED EDITION]

Foreword by RALPH G. NEWMAN

Southern Illinois University Press
Carbondale and Edwardsville

Previously published by Lincoln's New Salem Enterprise, Inc.

New edition published 1988 by Southern Illinois University Press,

Carbondale, IL 62901

Library of Congress Cataloging-in-Publication Data

Thomas, Benjamin Platt, 1902–1956.
    Lincoln's New Salem.

    Reprint. Originally published: Lincoln's
New Salem, Ill. : Lincoln's New Salem Enterprises, 1973.
    Includes index.
    1. Lincoln, Abraham, 1809–1865—Homes and haunts—
Illinois—New Salem (Sangamon County). 2. New Salem
(Sangamon County, Ill.)—History. 3. Lincoln, Abraham,
1809–1865—Museums, relics, etc.—Illinois—New Salem
(Sangamon County) I. Title.
E457.35.T47   1988   973.7'092'4   87-12988
ISBN 0-8093-1389-8 (pbk.)

Foreword

THIS is an American classic. It is a book written from the heart about the turning point in a great life. It was at New Salem that Abraham Lincoln for the first time learned to live with people. This was the first organized community in which he had a part. He learned here that there was great satisfaction in enjoying the good will and friendship of his neighbors. He also learned that if they liked and respected you, they would vote for you.

Carl Sandburg reminds us that in 1831, the year twenty-two-year old Abraham Lincoln floated a canoe down the Sangamon River to New Salem, it was a place of promise. All towns in this frontier state then were places of promise. New Salem had but a dozen families for its population; two hundred miles north on the shore of Lake Michigan in that same year was Chicago with a population of about the same size. Sandburg points out that both communities "had water transportation, outlets, tributary territory, yet one was to be only a phantom hamlet of memories and ghosts, a windswept hilltop kept as cherished haunts are kept."

Though New Salem "winked out," Illinois became a place of promise to Abraham Lincoln, and today, one hundred and forty-two years after he came to this state, the man and the place have become inseparable.

Benjamin Platt Thomas (1902–1956) was one of the great Lincoln students of the twentieth century. His one-volume biography of the Sixteenth President, published in 1952, is the best work of its kind and is universally acclaimed and accepted as the authoritative, compact work on the subject. He was the Executive Secretary of the Abraham Lincoln Association from 1932 to 1936 and in that position helped lay the groundwork for the *Collected Works of Abraham Lincoln*, which was completed by his successors. His *Portrait for Posterity: Lincoln and his Biographers*, (1947), is a charming book and unique in the field of Lincolniana. Benjamin Thomas was meticulous in his research and inspired in his writing. He was a friend of all who traveled along the Lincoln trail.

Lincoln's New Salem was originally issued as a publication of the Abraham Lincoln Association in 1934; reprinted in 1939, 1944, and 1947; and revised with the help of the late Harry E. Pratt and issued in a new edition in 1954 and reprinted in 1961 and 1966. This is the eighth edition of the work to be published.

RALPH G. NEWMAN

Preface

FOR many years the surroundings in which Lincoln spent his boyhood, youth, and early manhood were looked upon as drab, sordid, uninspiring; as an obstacle that he in some mysterious manner succeeded in surmounting. As time went on, however, historians saw the frontier as a major factor in molding our institutions and national character. And it also molded men. With this new conception of history came the realization that Lincoln, in large measure, was shaped by his frontier environment; that, while it made life hard for him, it also gave him strength, courage, and confidence.

Lincoln had less than a year of formal schooling. For the rest, he was self-made. He learned; he was not taught. What he read, he mastered; but he did not read widely. He learned principally by mingling with people and discussing affairs with them, by observation of their ways and their reactions—in short, from his environment.

This growing appreciation of the part that Lincoln's environment played in shaping him induced the

State of Illinois to undertake the restoration of the village of New Salem, and is our reason for describing its people, their occupations, interests, customs, religion, manner of life, and thought.

Some of New Salem's residents had important and easily recognized influence on Lincoln. Denton Offutt brought him to New Salem. Mentor Graham taught him grammar and mathematics, both of which were essential to his further development. Jack Kelso introduced him to Shakespeare and Burns. Jack Armstrong and his followers became his personal friends and political supporters. Others of the inhabitants touched his life at different points and even the humblest and most inconspicuous of them had some part in the making of the later, greater Lincoln. Lincoln's success as a politician and president, for example, was due in no small measure to the fact that he knew how the common man would think. This he learned in large part at New Salem, where he worked on common terms with the humblest of the villagers. He learned how and what Joshua Miller, the blacksmith, thought, how Bill Clary, the saloonkeeper, Martin Waddell, the hatter, and Alexander Ferguson, the cobbler, viewed things. He knew the common people because he had been one of them.

No other portion of Lincoln's life lends itself so readily to intensive study of his environment as do his six years at New Salem. His physical surroundings have been re-created. The names and occupations of practically all of his associates and something of the character of many of them are known. The village was small enough to make practicable a reasonably complete description of its people and its life.

Aside from its connection with Lincoln, New Salem is important as an example of a typical American pioneer village. There were hundreds like it. Some of them survived; others died, as it did. It is one of the few—perhaps the only one—whose founding, growth, and decline can be minutely traced.

Part One of this book is devoted to the history of New Salem. It tells who the inhabitants were, how they lived, how they looked on life. Since many of those most active in the village lived in outlying settlements, the account is not limited to the village, but provides a picture of the whole community. Part One sets the stage, so to speak, for Part Two, in which Lincoln's activities are discussed and the meaning of the New Salem years in his development is appraised. Part Three explains the growth of the Lincoln legend around the site of the lost town, and the changing conception of the significance of the frontier as a factor in Lincoln's life. It explains how New Salem came to be restored, the manner in which the facts about the old cabins were secured, how the furnishings were acquired, and the problems that had to be solved in the restoration.

The files of the *Sangamo Journal* have yielded new facts. The letters of Charles James Fox Clarke, who lived in and, later, near New Salem, published in the *Journal of the Illinois State Historical Society* for January 1930 but never used before in any book on New Salem, give a vivid picture of New Salem life. T. G. Onstot's *Pioneers of Menard and Mason Counties* and Peter Cartwright's *Autobiography* give the color of the pioneer days. County histories, reminiscences of old settlers, accounts of travelers, books and articles on pioneer life have been read. The records of land entries in Menard County, land transfers in New Salem, and the records of the Sangamon County Commissioners Court have been examined.

The discovery of a copy of William Dean Howells's *Life of Lincoln*, published in 1860 and corrected by Lincoln himself, enables us to write with assurance on several hitherto uncertain points. This copy was owned by Samuel C. Parks of Lincoln, Illinois. Parks, a native of Vermont, was educated at Indiana University and read law with the firm of Stuart and Edwards in Springfield. In 1848 he moved to Logan County, where he had many contacts with Lincoln. They were sometimes associated in the trial of cases in the Logan Circuit Court. Like Lincoln, Parks became a Republican. He spoke at Republican meetings in Logan County, and on one or two occasions introduced Lincoln when the latter spoke there. He worked for Lincoln's nomination as the

Republican candidate for president in 1860, and Lincoln later appointed him Associate Justice of the Supreme Court of Idaho. In the summer of 1860 Lincoln, at his request, read his copy of Howells and made corrections in the margins. Through the courtesy of Mr. Parks's son, Samuel C. Parks, Jr., of Cody, Wyoming, the Abraham Lincoln Association was permitted to examine this book and make photostatic copies of the pages on which Lincoln's corrections appear. In 1938 the Association republished the book in facsimile, showing Lincoln's corrections, and later the original copy was acquired by the Illinois State Historical Library.

The research work done by the Division of Architecture and Engineering of the State of Illinois in connection with the restoration of New Salem added to our knowledge of the village, especially with respect to the character and construction of the houses. This information, published in a mimeographed *Record of the Restoration of New Salem* by Joseph F. Booton, who had immediate charge of the research for the state, proved to be immensely valuable.

Anyone writing on New Salem must pay tribute to the Old Salem Lincoln League [1] of Petersburg, Illinois, for collecting and preserving information about the town and its residents. Their material, published in *Lincoln at New Salem* by Thomas P. Reep, has been freely drawn upon.

[1] Now the New Salem Lincoln League.

To the late Logan Hay, who was President of the Abraham Lincoln Association at the time this book was written, I shall always be grateful. Giving freely of his time to suggest improvements in style and content, he made this a better book than it would otherwise have been. Paul M. Angle, then head of the Illinois State Historical Library and now Director of the Chicago Historical Society, read the entire manuscript to its great benefit. George W. Bunn, Jr., who succeeded Mr. Hay as President of the Abraham Lincoln Association, also offered sound advice.

Margaret C. Norton, Archivist of the State of Illinois, loaned me material she had collected on Lincoln's activities in the State Legislature. The Herbert Georg Studio of Springfield furnished the photographs used by Romaine Proctor in drawing the illustrations. Margaret T. Davis drew the map of the New Salem community, and Mr. Proctor drew the map of the village.

To all state officials, and to all those who worked with them, we shall ever be grateful for the faithful reproduction of a pioneer town, which is also a unique memorial to Lincoln.

BENJAMIN P. THOMAS

Springfield, Illinois
January 2, 1954

CONTENTS

ILLUSTRATIONS

———◦•◦———

The drawings by ROMAINE PROCTOR *are from photographs
by the* HERBERT GEORG STUDIO, *Springfield, Illinois*

MAPS

LINCOLN'S NEW SALEM

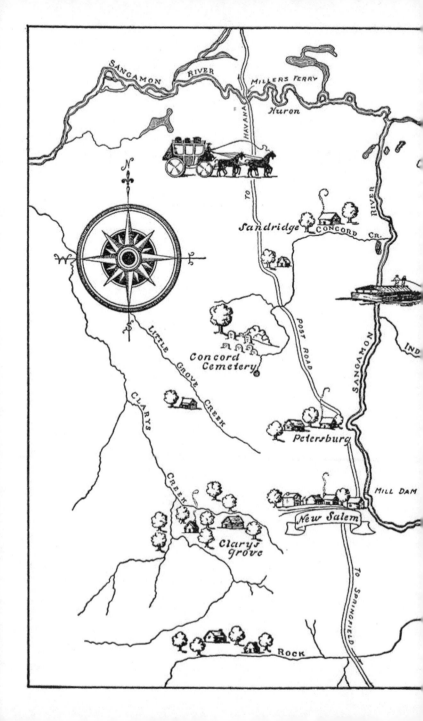

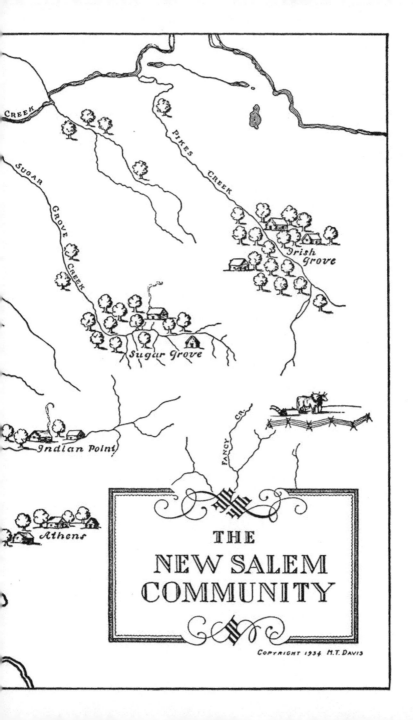

CREEK

SUGAR

PIKES CREEK

GROVE CREEK

Irish Grove

Sugar Grove

FANCY CR.

Indian Point

Athens

THE
NEW SALEM
COMMUNITY

COPYRIGHT 1934 M.T. DAVIS

PART ONE

New Salem

THE OUTSTANDING feature of Lincoln's life was his capacity for development. Neither a born genius nor a man of mediocre talents suddenly endowed with wisdom to guide the nation through the trials of civil war, he developed gradually, absorbing from his environment that which was useful and good, growing in character and mind. "How slowly, and yet by happily prepared steps, he came to his place," said Emerson.

No one seeing Lincoln at New Salem would have predicted for him the high place he was to reach in public life and world esteem; yet at New Salem many of the characteristics which were to make him great were in process of development, while others were present in rudimentary form.

In New Salem Lincoln made his reputation for physical prowess and began the development of his talents of leadership. There he served his apprenticeship in business, made his first venture into business on his own account, and established the reputation for square dealing that stuck to him through life. While there he had his one brief experience as a soldier, and held his first state and first Federal office. He learned surveying, acquired the elements of law, improved his knowledge of grammar, mathematics, and literature, and made his first formal efforts at speech-making and debate. There he made his first venture into politics and formed his first enduring friendships. He came to New Salem an aimless pioneer youth; he left with an aroused ambition. Because of the friendship these New Salem people showed him, he would never afterward believe otherwise than that people, fundamentally, are trustworthy and good.

The village of New Salem—Lincoln's home from 1831 to 1837—was founded in 1829 by James Rutledge and John M. Camron. The former was born in South Carolina in 1781. Early in his life his family moved to Georgia. From there they moved to Tennessee, thence to Kentucky. There Rutledge married and had several children, among them a daughter, Ann. In 1813 he and his family moved to White County, Illinois. He was a man of medium height, quiet, dignified, sincerely religious, and fairly well educated. Camron, a native of Georgia, ten years younger than Rutledge, was a nephew of Rutledge's wife. He accompanied his uncle on his migration from Georgia to White County. A man of great physical strength, a millwright by trade, Camron was an ordained Cumberland Presbyterian preacher as well.

In 1825 or 1826 Rutledge and Camron moved again, this time to Concord Creek, in Sangamon County, about seven miles north of the site of New Salem. There they entered land and planned to build a mill. But the volume of water in the creek was insufficient, and after an extensive search for a suitable site, on July 19, 1828, Camron entered a tract of land on the Sangamon River. There they were assured of a steady flow, so they applied to the State Legislature for permission to build a dam.

Anticipating favorable action, they left Concord Creek, probably in the fall of 1828, built new homes on the bluff above the river; and moved in before cold weather came. On January 22, 1829, the Legislature granted them permission to build the dam. Its construction was begun at once, farmers from the surrounding country furnishing oxen and horses to haul rocks with which to fill the wooden bins that had been placed in the stream.

The dam completed, a combination sawmill and gristmill, of solid frame construction, was erected beside it. The gristmill was enclosed and set out over the stream. The sawmill, with its old-fashioned upright saw, had a roof, but was open on the sides, and stood on the west bank. A wooden trestle connected both mills with the steep bank.

Soon the gristmill was drawing trade from miles around. On busy days thirty or forty horses would be tied to the trees on the steep hillside, "their heads forty-five degrees above their hams." In the fall of 1829 Samuel Hill and John McNeil, attracted by the growing business of the mill, opened a store on the hill above, at the point where the road from Springfield, ascending the slope from the south, curved toward the east. Soon a "grocery" or saloon, kept by William Clary, was dispensing liquor on the bluff.[1] Now, while waiting for their grain to be ground, men could stock up with supplies and lounge about the store, or drink and play "old sledge" at the grocery. When the boys were sent to mill they whiled away the time fishing or swimming or with feats of strength and skill on the bluff.

A mill, a store, and a grocery were the usual beginnings of a pioneer village, and as the place became a center of trade Rutledge and Camron resolved to lay out a town and sell lots. The ridge above the mill provided a beautiful site. Extending westward from the river, it widens and gradually merges with the prairie. At the bottom of its steep southern slope, Green's

---

[1] "Grocery" was the frontier term for a saloon.

Rocky Branch ran eastward to the Sangamon. On the north the ridge sloped down sharply to another little stream, later called Bale's Branch, which also flowed to the river. The steep bluff at the eastern end of the ridge deflects the Sangamon, flowing from the southeast, to the north. Groves of virgin timber crowned the rolling hills of the vicinity and lined the watercourses.

On October 23, 1829, Reuben Harrison, a surveyor whom Rutledge and Camron had employed, planned and laid out a town on the ridge. It was the first town platted within the limits of the present Menard County. The proprietors named it New Salem.

On December 24 the first lot was sold to James Pantier for $12.50. Ten days later Pantier paid $7.00 for a second lot, adjoining his original purchase.[2] On Christmas Day, 1829, a post office was established, with Samuel Hill as postmaster. Previously the people in that part of the county got their mail at Springfield, some twenty miles away.

In 1830 Henry Onstot, a cooper, moved from Sugar Grove and built a shop and residence in the southeastern part of the village near the bluff. James and Rowan Herndon opened a store. Clary established a ferry, thereby making the village more accessible from the east and extending its trading area in that

---

[2] His first purchase was lot four south of Main Street in the first survey, his second was lot three, adjoining it on the south.

direction. The County Commissioners allowed him the following rates:

For each man and horse	$ .12½
For each footman	.06¼
For each single horse	.06¼
For each head of neat cattle	.03
For each head of sheep	.02
For each road wagon and team	.50
For each two horse wagon and	
pleasure carriage	.25

When the river was out of its banks, or before sunrise or after sunset, he could charge double these amounts.

In 1831 the village continued to grow. In August, John Allen, a young physician from Vermont, bought Pantier's lots and built a house across the street from Hill's store. Allen had received his medical degree from Dartmouth College Medical School three years before, and came west to seek a climate that might benefit his health. Early in September, Denton Offutt, who had stopped in New Salem in April when the flatboat that he was taking to New Orleans stranded on the mill dam, returned to the village, opened a store on the bluff near Clary's grocery, and rented the mill.[3] Late in July came

[3] Offutt bought lot fourteen north of Main Street in the first survey from William Batterton on September 2, 1831. Batterton had purchased it from Camron on January 14. When the village was resurveyed in 1932, it was found that Offutt's store was not located on this lot, but a short distance to the north.

Main Street, New Salem, Showing Samuel Hill's Residence, the Hill-McNeil Store, the Lincoln-Berry Store, and Peter Lukins's House

Abraham Lincoln, a young man who had worked for Offutt on the flatboat, and who now joined him at New Salem to clerk in the store and run the mill.

The same year David Whary purchased a lot in the eastern part of town.[4] Henry Sinco, the constable, opened a saloon.[5] Peter Lukins built a house and had a cobbler's shop in one of its two rooms. George Warburton opened the town's fourth store and obtained a license to sell drinks. Later that year he sold out to two brothers from Virginia, St. Clair and Isaac P. Chrisman. In November, Isaac Chrisman succeeded Hill as postmaster; but he and his brother sold their store to Reuben Radford shortly afterward and left town, and Hill again took over the post office. As immigrants came to the Sangamon country, Rutledge converted his house into a tavern and built an addition for guests.

Settlement in Illinois progressed from the south northward. The northern part of Sangamon County began to attract settlers about 1819, and at the time New Salem was founded the surrounding country, within a radius of ten or fifteen miles, already contained scattered farms and several smaller settlements. West of the river the nucleus of the population was the

[4] December 19, 1831, Whary paid $16 for lot twelve in the first survey. The record does not show whether it was north or south of Main Street.

[5] On September 8, 1831, he paid $30 for lot five north of Main Street in the first survey. October 25, he paid $10 for lot one, nearby. His tavern license was issued on December 6, 1830.

Armstrong-Clary-Greene-Potter-Watkins-McHenry-Kirby clan. These families had intermarried in Tennessee, Kentucky, and southern Illinois as they gradually trekked north. In 1819 John Clary, who married Rhoda Armstrong while they were living in Tennessee, came to Sangamon County and settled in the grove that came to bear his name. He was the first settler within the area of the present Menard County. He was followed, in the early twenties, by most of the other members of the clan, who migrated north in groups.

These families, settling in and around Clary's Grove and Little Grove, southwest of the site of New Salem, and along Rock Creek, to the south, dominated that part of the country. Early in the thirties most of the Armstrongs and Clarys moved northward to Concord and Sand Ridge. East of the river, in Sugar Grove, Irish Grove, Athens, and Indian Point, there was less relationship between the families.

New Salem, from the time it was founded until 1833 or 1834, was the trading-point of all these settlements. The village and its surrounding area were really one community. No account of the village can be adequate unless it treats also of these outlying places, for many of those who were important in the life of the village lived outside it.

At the time New Salem was founded few villages of any size existed farther north. Peoria had been estab-

lished, and at Dixon's Ferry, where the trail from
Peoria to the lead mines at Galena crossed the Rock
River, and at other points along that trail there were
clusters of cabins. At Hennepin there was a fur-trading
post. Chicago had a population of about 100 people,
living in a few log cabins huddled about Fort Dearborn.
For sixty or seventy miles north of Sangamon County
there were from two to six settlers to the square mile.
Farther north were areas of trackless prairie, still
roamed at times by hostile Indians, whose presence de-
terred settlers from coming too far north. As late as
1837 the country between Bloomington and Decatur
was very sparsely settled. Springfield, twenty miles
southeast of New Salem, contained about 500 people in
1830. Settlers built in the groves and along the streams,
where timber was available for cabins, fences, and fuel,
where water for stock could be had, and where the land
could be more easily broken. Away from timber the
treeless, sun-baked prairie was almost uninhabited.[6]

Throughout the state, inns were to be found only
in the larger villages, and along the more traveled
roads. A traveler from Chicago to New Salem in 1835

[6] The population of Illinois in 1830 was 157,445; that of
Sangamon County, the area of which was twice what it is today,
was 12,960, or about seven to the square mile. By 1840 the population of the state was 476,183, that of Sangamon County, reduced
to its present size, was 14,716, about seventeen to the square mile.
The population of Menard County in 1840 was 4,431, about eight
to the square mile.

recorded that "the fare along the road was rather poor. We stopped one night at a house or rather it was a small cabin (one room only), where we were rather crowded there being twenty-seven lodgers, the landlord said he had often lodged that number we *put out* early in the morning feeling thankful that we had not been lost in the crowd."

The greatest need of central Illinois was adequate transportation. The soil was rich, but it was difficult to get crops to market. Under "Hints to Immigrants" the *Sangamo Journal* of February 9, 1832, gave an impressive description of the difficulties of travel. "In the spring, the bottom-lands are overflowed, the channels of all streams are full, and the travelling in any direction is impeded, and sometimes wholly stopped, by high waters.—The roads, generally speaking, are new; because the great channels of trade are not yet settled. Population is rapidly increasing, and trade fluctuating from point to point; the courses of roads are consequently often changed, before a permanent route is adopted. Few roads, therefore, have become so fixed, as to their location, as to have been beaten by travel, and improved by art; and the traveller who ventures out in the spring, may expect to be obliged to wade through mire and water—ancle deep, knee deep, and peradventure deeper than that. But the spring is, for the same reason, the most eligible season for travelling by water.

. . . The steam boat glides without interruption from port to port, ascends even the smallest rivers, and finds her way to places far distant from the ordinary channels of navigation. . . . The *traveller by water* meets with no delay, while the hapless wight, who bestrides an ugly nag, is wading through ponds and quagmires, enjoying the delights of log bridges and wooden causeways, and vainly invoking the name of McAdam, as he plunges deeper and deeper into mire and misfortune." In the autumn, on the other hand, streams became dry or shallow and roads were the better routes.

With roads poor and frequently impassable, the future of New Salem, and that of the Sangamon country as well, was believed to depend primarily on the possibility of making the river navigable for light-draft steamboats. A hundred and twenty years ago the volume of water in the Sangamon was greater than it is today, and great hopes were entertained of its navigability. On February 2, 1832, the *Journal* observed: "It would be folly, perhaps, ever to anticipate for our village [Springfield] advantages from steam boat navigation equal to those which St. Louis derived from that source. Yet such an anticipation can not be deemed more chimerical than was the project of running steam boats from the mouth of the Ohio to St. Louis in 1817."

In the spring of 1832 the *Talisman*, a small cabin steamer from Cincinnati, actually managed to ascend the Sangamon as far as Portland Landing, a point near Springfield several miles above New Salem. "The result," declared the *Journal* on March 29, "has clearly demonstrated the practicability of navigating the river by steamboats of a proper size ; and by the expenditure of 2,000 dollars in removing the logs and drifts and standing timber, a steam boat of 80 tons burthen will make the trip in two days from Beardstown to this place." On May 10, 1832, announcement was made that the steamboat *Sylph* would soon leave Cincinnati for Springfield, "and that, if the stage of water in the Sangamon permits, and business on the river will justify it, she will continue to run on the river during the ensuing season."

The prospect of cheap and steady transportation started a boom. More settlers came. Prospective towns were laid out at strategic points along the Sangamon ; and the *Journal* congratulated "our farmers, our mechanics, our merchants, and professional men, for the rich harvest in prospect." The future of the country seemed assured.

Anticipation of New Salem's becoming a thriving river town caused an inrush of new settlers ; and in 1832 the village reached its peak. Isaac Burner and Isaac Guliher built houses.[7] Joshua Miller, a blacksmith

[7] Burner paid $10 for lots two and three south of Main Street in the second survey on October 25, 1832.

and wagonmaker, and his brother-in-law, Jack Kelso, erected a cabin and blacksmith shop, which was soon one of the busiest places in town. From morning until night Miller's anvil clanged as he forged ox shoes, horseshoes, implements, and household fittings.[8]

Francis Regnier, a young doctor from Ohio, bought the house that Sinco had used for a saloon, refitted it, and lived and had his office in its single room.[9] Martin Waddell built a house and made hats and caps for the community. Philemon Morris built a residence and tanyard. Robert Johnson, a wheelwright and cabinetmaker, settled in New Salem and made spinning-wheels, wagon wheels, and furniture.[1]

The population of New Salem, like that of many pioneer towns, was ever changing as settlers came,

[8] Miller bought lots nine and ten north of Main Street in the second survey, and a piece of land adjoining to the north, on November 17, 1832. The purchase price was $25.

[9] Regnier paid Sinco $20 for the west half of lot one north of Main Street in the first survey on October 10, 1832.

[1] The following land transactions, not mentioned in the text, were consummated in 1832. On January 6, Edmund Greer bought lot one south of Main Street (survey not given) from Robert Melton for $50. The same day, Hill bought lot four north of Main Street in the first survey for $16. This was the lot on which his store was situated. May 9, John MacNamar paid $10 for the east half of lot five north of Main Street in the first survey. Alexander Trent bought lot thirteen (no further description given) on August 27 for $50. On November 2 Baxter B. Berry paid $10 for the east half of lots seven and eight south of Main Street in the second survey. On the same day Hill sold the west forty feet of his lot to George Spears for $26.66⅔. Robert McNeeley, Jonathan Dunn, a millwright, Johnson Elmore, and Caleb Carman, a shoemaker, were other New Salem residents.

The Interior of Dr. Francis Regnier's House

stayed a few months, and moved on. Dr. Jason Duncan lived there for a short time, then moved to Warsaw, Illinois. Charles James Fox Clarke, a young man from New Hampshire, boarded at the tavern for a while, then moved to a nearby farm. In the summer of 1832 William F. Berry and Abraham Lincoln bought the Herndon brothers' store; and a little later, as the town continued to grow, they bought out Reuben Radford. This left Hill as their only competitor; for in the spring Offutt had closed his store, given up the mill, and moved away. In the autumn Jacob Bale, a Kentuckian, bought the mill. Bill Clary moved to Texas and Alexander Trent bought his grocery. When Lukins and Warburton founded the town of Petersburg, two miles down the river, in 1832, Alexander Ferguson moved into Lukins's house, took his place as shoemaker, and soon had a thriving business. Farmers took their hides to Morris to be tanned, then brought the leather and the measurements of the family feet to Ferguson. Two or three weeks later they would come back with a two-bushel sack and take home twelve or fifteen pairs of shoes.

The tavern changed hands several times. November 26, 1832, Camron sold it to Nelson Alley for $200; and in December 1834 Alley sold it to Henry Onstot, the cooper. Onstot operated it for about a year, then built a new house and cooper shop in the western part of town and sold the tavern to Michael Keltner. Clary, James Richardson, John Ferguson, brother of the cobbler, Alexander Trent, and Jacob Bale and his son Hardin were successive owners of the ferry.

For four years after the coming of the *Talisman* in 1832, rumors of the navigation of the river recurred at intervals. Most of the villagers still believed it could and would be navigated; but the more practical began to doubt. Settlers continued to take up the rich land of the surrounding country, but by the spring of 1833 New Salem's growth had stopped. Few new settlers came that year, and some old ones moved away. The Camrons went to Fulton County. James Rutledge moved to a farm on Sand Ridge.² Lincoln and Berry, disillusioned in their mercantile venture, sold out to Alexander and Martin S. Trent. On September 17, 1835, Mathew S. Marsh, who lived two miles southwest of New Salem, wrote to his brother: "You ask is there a prospect of my place growing rapidly. I suppose you mean New Salem—No; that stopped two years since." On the whole, however, the village held its own until 1836.

New Salem was on the road from Springfield to Havana, and in April 1836 a stage line was established

² Rutledge moved to Sand Ridge early in 1833. He died there on December 3, 1835. His widow and her family, except her son David, moved to Fulton County in 1836. From there they moved to Iowa.

on that road. A four-horse post coach, owned by Tracy
and Reny, was scheduled to leave Springfield every
Wednesday morning at six o'clock. It passed through
Sangamon Town, New Salem, Petersburg, Huron, Havana, Lewistown, Canton, Knoxville, and Monmouth,
and was due at Yellow Banks (the present Oquawka),
on the Mississippi 130 miles from Springfield, on Saturday at noon. It was scheduled to begin the return
trip the same day, arrive at New Salem Tuesday morning, and reach Springfield that afternoon. More often
than not, however, it was hours or even days late; and
in very bad weather it did not run at all. The fare for
through passengers was nine dollars; for way passengers, six and a quarter cents a mile. Since it cost about
a dollar and a half to get to Springfield, Lincoln sel-
dom rode the stage in his numerous trips back and
forth.

In the spring of 1835 Samuel Hill built a carding-
machine and storehouse for wool west of Dr. Regnier's
house. He advertised in the *Journal* of April 24 that he
would commence carding by May 1. "The machines are
nearly new and in first rate order, and I do not hesitate
to say, the best work will be done. Just bring your wool
in good order and their will be no mistake." The cogs of
the machine were made of hickory wood; and a yoke of
oxen, hitched to a forty-foot wheel, supplied the motive
power. "Every person kept sheep in those days," wrote

T. G. Onstot, the cooper's son, "and took the wool to
the machine where it was carded by taking toll out of
the wool or sometimes they would pay for it. They commenced bringing in wool in May and by June the building would be full. It was amusing to see the sacks of all

THE HILL-MCNEIL STORE

sorts and sizes and sometimes old petticoats. For every
ten pounds of wool they would bring a gallon of grease,
mostly in old gourds. Large thorns were used to pin the
packages together."

Hill was the town's leading businessman. While
other stores failed, his prospered as long as the village
survived. On September 4, 1832, his partnership with

McNeil was dissolved by mutual consent, and Hill continued in business alone. On July 28, 1835, he married Parthena Nance of Rock Creek.[3] Shortly before their marriage he built a two-story house beside the store. Hot-tempered and shrewd, Hill was thrifty to the point of stinginess. The Reverend Peter Cartwright, his inveterate enemy, claimed that he had always believed that Hill had no soul until he put a quarter to his lips and his soul "came up to get it." Hill's store was the center of village life. Throughout the day shoppers and gossipers came and went, or lounged on its porch, reading mail, exchanging news, or talking crops or politics. On election day the polls were located either there or at the Lincoln-Berry store or the tavern.

At the height of its prosperity New Salem had a population of some twenty-five families, with twenty-five or thirty log or frame structures, among them the saw- and gristmill, the tavern, three or four general stores, the grocery, the cooper shop, the blacksmith shop, and the tannery. It had no church, but services were held in the schoolhouse, across the Rocky Branch to the south of the village, near the cemetery, and in the homes of the inhabitants.

[3] September 4, 1834, Hill bought back from Spears for $50 the west forty feet of lot four. He had sold this to Spears in 1832. On April 8, 1833, he bought lot two north of Main Street in the second survey for $100.

It was a typical pioneer town. Almost everything needed was produced in the village or the surrounding countryside. Cattle, sheep, and goats grazed on the hillsides. Hogs rooted in the woods and wallowed in the dust and mud of the road. Gardens were planted about the houses, and wheat, oats, corn, cotton, and tobacco grew in the surrounding fields. In August 1834 C. J. F. Clarke described conditions to his relatives in the East. "I have been requested," he wrote, "by all those that I have recd letters from to write what the people live in, what they live on etc. I will tell you. I should judge that nine tenths of them live in log houses and cabbins the other tenth either in brick or framed houses. The people generally have large farmes and have not thought so much of fine buildings as they have of adding land to land, they are now however beginning to build better houses. Many a rich farmer lives in a house not half so good as your old hogs pen and not any larger. We live generally on bacon, eggs, bread, coffee. Potatoes are not much used, ten bushels is a large crop and more than is used in a family in a year. Sweet potatoes are raised here very easy. The wheat crop is very good, corn is very promising mother wishes to know what kind of trees grow here. We have all kinds except pine and hemlock, houses are built of white oak and black walnut and some linn. Almost all kinds of fruit grows here spontaneously among them are the crab apple, cherry, two or three kinds of plums, black and white haw, gooseberrys, etc., etc. The black walnut is a beautiful tree the wood of which is very much like mahogany. There is a considerable quantity of cotton raised here but none for expotation. Tobacco grows well here, etc. etc."

Sunflowers bloomed profusely on the prairie. In the spring and summer, bass, sunfish, catfish, and suckers could be caught in the river near the dam. Sometimes there was good seining below the mill, and occasionally fish could be gigged. Wild turkeys abounded in the woods, and deer, while becoming scarce, could still be had. Quail, prairie hens, ducks, and wild geese were plentiful. Prairie wolves, a small species about the size of a fox, though rapidly being exterminated, were still a menace to sheep.

Although the neighboring farmhouses were in many cases crude, the buildings in New Salem were fairly substantial and comfortable structures. Most of them were log houses rather than cabins. The frontiersman drew a distinction between these two types of structures. Peck's *New Guide for Emigrants* (1837) says: "A *log house*, in western parlance, differs from a cabin, in the logs being hewn on two sides to an equal thickness, before raising; in having a framed and shingled roof, a brick or stone chimney, windows, tight floors, and are fre-

The Interior of Peter Lukins's House

quently clapboarded on the outside and plastered within. A log house, thus finished, costs more than a framed one."

All the houses in New Salem, except Hill's residence, were one story high. Occasionally they had a loft above. With few exceptions they had only one or two rooms. Writing of the early one-room house, Onstot said: "At meal time it was all kitchen. On rainy days when all the neighbors came there to relate their exploits, how many deer and turkeys they had killed, it was the sitting room. On Sunday when the young men all dressed up in their jeans, and the young ladies in their best bow dresses, it was all parlor. At night it was all bed-room."

Houses built before the coming of Joshua Miller, the blacksmith, had leather or wooden hinges and wooden latches and locks. In those built later, these fittings were often of iron. Those antedating the mill had puncheon floors and were of cruder construction than those for which planks for floors, ceilings, and siding could be sawed at the mill. Fireplaces were made of stone or brick; chimneys of stone or of the "cat and clay" type—logs and sticks chinked with mud or plaster. When a chimney was built on the inside of a cabin, between two rooms, it was invariably made of stone because of the danger of fire. On windy days persons with "cat and clay" chimneys had to go outside frequently and look at them to be sure they were not on fire.

Roofs were built of clapboards or shingles—sometimes called "shakes"—held in place by nails, or by logs, known as "weight poles," laid across them. Walls were of logs, notched and fitted together at the corners and chinked with sticks and plaster made of mud and hair. Doors were of frame construction. Those with wooden latches had buckskin latchstrings, which were tied to the latch and passed outside through a hole above it. When only friends were about "the latchstring was always out," but in time of danger it could be pulled in through the hole.

One of New Salem's stores was of frame construction. Hill's store, his residence, and Offutt's store had porches. Almost all New Salem structures had glass windows, for there was a glazier at Springfield at least as early as 1832, and glass and nails were available at St. Louis even before that time. Usually windows were situated near the fireplace, where cooking was done and near which most family activities were carried on. Because the prevailing winter winds came from the north and west, windows were almost always cut in the south or east walls. The first house in the New Salem neighborhood to have glass windows, instead of the greased-paper variety, was that of George Spears, built in 1830 at Clary's Grove. Spears's house was also the first to be built of brick. The mud for the bricks was trampled by oxen. None of the houses in New Salem was of brick, although there were some brick houses close by.

On the bluff above the river the New Salem settlers were more exposed to the elements than their neighbors in the lowlands. Clarke recorded that in the summer of 1835 "a violent tornado past over this part of the country and blew down all the fences and destroyed much timber." Biting winds swept the hill in wintertime. Occasionally snow sifted down the wide chimneys, deadened the coals in the fireplace, and spread a thin white covering on the floor. At times the wind drove the stinging wood smoke back into the cabins. On bitter winter days, even with a roaring fire, the unplastered cabins were often cold.

The winter of 1830–1—the winter of the "deep snow"—was especially severe. In December a raging storm piled up the snow three feet deep on the level. Then came rain, which froze and formed a crust of ice. On top of this was deposited a layer of fine, light snow. The storm ended with a cutting northwest wind, which drove the snow across the prairie in a blinding, choking swirl. Tracks made one day were obliterated by the next. Feed was still in the fields, and on some of the newer farms sheds had not yet been built for the stock. The crust would support a man, but horses broke through. Deer became a helpless prey for wolves as their

sharp hoofs cut through the crust and prevented them
from running. Day after day the thermometer rose no
higher than twelve below zero, and for three weeks there
was no thaw. For nine weeks snow covered the country-

HENRY ONSTOT'S COOPER SHOP AND RESIDENCE.
THE COOPER SHOP IS THE ONLY ORIGINAL
BUILDING AT NEW SALEM

side. When it melted all the streams were swollen out of
their banks.

The winter of 1836–7 was also hard. That was the
year of the "sudden freeze," when a quick shift of the
wind caused the temperature to take a precipitate drop.
It had been raining for some time, and water and slush
turned almost instantly to ice. Geese and chickens were

frozen to the ground. Several people, caught on the open prairie, died. Clarke told of a drove of 900 hogs that were overtaken on the prairie four miles from house or timber. "The men left the hogs and made out to get to a house alive although they were very much frozen one was not expected to live. The hogs piled themselves up into a heap and remained there three days before the[y] could be got away and then they were hauled on sleds, twenty only were found dead." Washington Crowder, riding into Springfield, attempted to dismount at a store, "but was unable to move, his overcoat holding him as firmly as though it had been made of sheet iron. He then called for help, and two men come out, who tried to lift him off, but his clothes were frozen to the saddle, which they ungirthed, and then carried man and saddle to the fire and thawed them asunder." Sun and rain, wind, snow, and cold were important factors in the lives of the pioneers.

Most settlers in the New Salem vicinity made their living from the soil. To break the hard-baked, untilled prairie, covered with long, thick-rooted, matted grass, with oxen—sometimes several yoke—was arduous labor for the strongest men. Twenty to forty acres was all that could be broken in a year. James McGrady Rutledge, of Sand Ridge, owned three yoke of oxen, which he hired out to break land. Even after the land had been broken, plowing was hard work. The plows had steel shares; but the moldboards were made of wood, and scoured poorly in the sticky soil. A plow with a long, sloping moldboard was best suited to the hard or muddy prairie loam. The settlers cultivated corn by hand with a hoe or a "bull tongue" plow. Grain was cut with a sickle, threshed with a flail, and winnowed by tossing it in a sheet so that the wind would blow away the chaff. A few settlers, like Tom Watkins of Clary's Grove, tried stock-raising on an extensive scale, letting their stock run at large on the prairie.

The women worked harder than the men. Clarke wrote that "a man can get corn and pork enough to last his family a fortnight for a single day's work, while a woman must keep scrubbing from morning till night the same in this country as in any other." Women prepared the food, bore and cared for the children, spun thread, wove cloth and made clothes, churned the butter, made soap and candles, and performed most of the humble, humdrum, necessary tasks. An English traveler noted that central Illinois was "a hard country for women and cattle."

Marriageable girls did not stay single long. Clarke told of one who arrived from the East in June and by August had "had no less than four suitors, . . . three widowers and one old batchelor." A man often outlived two wives, and sometimes three, or even four. Families were large, and babies came in annual crops. James

Rutledge had ten children, and Camron was the father of eleven girls. Mathew S. Marsh, writing from New Salem to his brother in 1835, complained that he had "one objection to marrying in this State and that is, the women have such an everlasting number of children, twelve is the least number that can be counted on." "Granny" Spears of Clary's Grove, a little old woman whose chin and nose nearly met, officiated at more than half the births in the community. "When weaned, usually by the almanac, youngsters began to eat cornbread, biscuits, and pot likker like grownups. The fittest survived and the rest 'the Lord seen fitten to take away.' " [4]

Cooking was done over the open fire, sometimes on a "flat oven," or in a "Dutch oven"; and with skillet, frying-pan, iron pot, and kettle. Stoves were unknown, and matches were just coming into use. The basis of the diet was corn meal, prepared in every way from mush to "corn dodgers," the latter being often hard enough "to split a board or fell a steer at forty feet." This was supplemented by lye hominy, vegetables, milk, pork, fish, and fowl. Honey was generally used in place of sugar. In summer grapes, berries, and fruit were added to this fare. The women made preserves, but most families used them only on special occasions or when company came. Ned Potter had a sugar camp and Mrs.

[4] R. Carlyle Buley, "Pioneer Health and Medical Practice in the Old Northwest," in the *Mississippi Valley Historical Review*, XX, 497 ff.

Potter's maple sugar "was legal tender for all debts."

Men wore cotton, flax, or tow-linen shirts, and pants of the same material or of jean or buckskin. In winter they wore hats or caps of wool or fur, sometimes with the tail of the animal dangling down behind; while in summer plaited hats of wheat straw, oats, or rye were the style. Boots and shoes were supplanting the moccasins formerly worn by both sexes, although moccasins could still be seen. Women were supplementing their dresses of wool, flannel, and flax with cotton and calico clothes. Cotton handkerchiefs, sunbonnets and straw hats were all used for feminine headgear. Children were often clad only in a long tow-linen shirt. In summer most of them—and sometimes their elders as well—went barefoot.

Each family produced most of what it used, although the presence of craftsmen in the village indicates some division of labor. But even craftsmen had gardens, and some of them bought farms; while farmers occupied the winter months with some sort of handicraft, producing articles for personal use or for sale. Almost every family kept a cow. Beside the houses gigantic woodpiles mounted during summer and fall, and dwindled as winter passed. Rain barrels caught the "soft" water that dripped from eaves. Lye for soap-making was leeched from wood ashes in hoppers in back yards. Drinking-water was obtained from wells, one of which was dug beside the Rutledge tavern and another near the Lincoln-Berry store.

Furniture was of the simple pioneer sort. Some of it had been brought from former homes, often with great difficulty; other pieces were homemade or fashioned by Robert Johnson in New Salem. Poor families had tables made of puncheons or unplaned boards, crude chairs, and "scaffold" beds, the framework for the latter being made by erecting a forked upright in a corner of a cabin about six feet from either wall and laying a pole from the upright to each wall. Families of moderate means had rush-seat chairs, cord and trundle beds, chests of drawers of plain but skillful workmanship. The boys were delegated to keep the woodbox, always found beside the fireplace, filled with logs. Corner cupboards were adorned with glass and chinaware. For those who could afford them, Seth Thomas clocks were the style. Rifles and shotguns hung on wooden pegs or brackets, or on deer or cow horns, over doors and on the walls. Tongs, spurs, bootjacks, candle molds hung beside the mantels. At night candles in brass or iron holders shed soft light through the rooms.

Merchants stocked their shelves with dry goods, furs, mittens, seeds, hides, tallow, lard, bacon, cheese, butter, beeswax, honey, eggs, hops, vegetables, firearms and ammunition, saddles, ox yokes, tools. In every store barrels of liquor stood along the wall. A few traders bought commodities from the farmers and sold them in St. Louis and New Orleans; and occasionally a farmer, having accumulated a surplus, loaded it on a raft or flatboat and floated down the Sangamon to Beardstown, thence down the Illinois and Mississippi to St. Louis, or even to New Orleans. The few commodities brought from afar—sugar, salt, coffee—came by boat from New Orleans or Cincinnati to St. Louis or Beardstown, and from there were distributed overland.

Some money came into the village through trade and some was brought by immigrants, but for the most part money was scarce and of uncertain value. Currency was chiefly bank notes, issued by banks good, bad, and indifferent, which passed at various discounts depending on the reputation of the bank of issue. Counterfeit notes were common. Trade was carried on largely through long-term credit. A man would bring his wool, for instance, to Hill's wool house, and instead of cash would receive a credit at Hill's store. He would draw on this from time to time throughout the year. Another individual might be "carried" by Hill until he sold his crops. The craftsmen of the village exchanged their wares for products of the farms and struck a balance with the farmers at the end of the year. Dr. Allen accepted dressed hogs, bacon, and lard in payment of bills, barrelled up his products, and shipped them to Beardstown and St. Louis.

Writing of the people of the West generally and of Illinois in particular, Peck said (1834) : "They have much plain, blunt, but sincere hospitality. Emigrants who come amongst them with a disposition to be pleased with the people and country,—to make no invidious comparisons,—and to assume no airs of distinction,—but to become amalgamated with the people . . . will be welcome." This characterization held true for the people who lived in and around New Salem. They were of the third wave of migration, having been preceded by the roving hunters and trappers and the restless squatters who stayed a few months and moved on. They were mostly farmers, many of them with some stock and capital, who bought land, or hoped to do so soon. They were home-builders who expected to remain and eventually to attain to a standard of living comparable to that of the regions whence they came. They too were restless, however, and many of them moved on, hoping to find better locations farther west.

The backbone of the community was the Southern pioneer element, represented by the Clarys, Armstrongs, Kirbys, Watkins, Potters, Rutledges, Camrons, and Greenes. The Chrismans were Virginians; Peter Lukins and his brother Gregory came from Kentucky; the Grahams and Onstots from Kentucky and Tennessee; the Berrys from Virginia through Tennessee and Indiana.

Interspersed with the predominant Southern element were a few Yankees—C. J. F. Clarke and Mathew S. Marsh, who entered land southwest of New Salem, and Dr. Allen, who represented the New England reformer type. Sam Hill came from New Jersey, John McNeil from New York, and Dr. Regnier, who was of French extraction, from Marietta, Ohio. The Southerners came by families; the Yankees and Easterners were individuals, who left their families to seek health, wealth, or adventure.

Like Westerners in general, the people of New Salem were young, enthusiastic, self-reliant, willing to take a chance. Equality of opportunity was in large degree a fact, and courage, endurance, and ingenuity were the requisites of success. Wealth, "kin and kin-in-law didn't count a cuss." Government was of, by, and for the people, with public opinion a most effective force.

There were two elements in the place: a happy-go-lucky, rough and roistering group, typified by the Clary's Grove boys, and men of a more serious turn, like Allen, Rutledge, Onstot, Regnier, and Graham. But no sharp social lines were drawn. Preacher and ne'er-do-well, doctor and laborer took part together in the village life. Grocery keeper and temperance advocate; farmer, craftsman, merchant; Yankee and Southerner rubbed elbows with one another. Diverse types were represented in the groups that idled at the stores. Discussions in such groups brought out conflicting opinions and differences in points of view. Men learned what other men were thinking.

Most notorious of the roistering, sporting crowd were the boys from Clary's Grove. They were always up to mischief of some sort. "They trimmed the manes and tails of horses, cut girths, put stones under saddles so as to cause riders to be thrown mounting." Favorite sports of this crowd were cockfighting, gander-pulling, and wrestling. The cockpit stood across the road from Clary's grocery, and the gander-pulling ground was at the eastern end of town, along the bluff. In this sport a tough old gander, its neck thoroughly greased, was tied, head down, to a limb of a tree. Then the contestants rode at full speed under the limb, and the one who could snap off the gander's head as he dashed by got the bird.

On the frontier men settled their disputes with fists, feet, and teeth as often as they resorted to the courts; or fought first and sued each other afterward. Sometimes they fought for the sheer love of fighting. Sam Hill, a small man himself, once offered a set of china dishes to John Ferguson, who had considerable local renown as a "scrapper," if he would whip Jack Armstrong, with whom Hill had had a quarrel. Ferguson accepted and, being larger than Armstrong, finally won; but he took such punishment that he later declared that the dishes would have been dear at half the price. On one occasion two incorrigible enemies fought out their differences on the far side of the river while the whole population watched from the bluff. Finally, when both men were down, a party crossed the river and pulled them apart. One of them was so severely beaten that he died of his hurts within a year.

But these ultra-virile aspects of the community life should not be overstressed. T. G. Onstot, relating the story of this fight, described it as typical of the frontier civilization of that day, but he added: "Many of the old citizens never had to contend with its barbaric customs. Only those who trained in that school were subject to its conditions." In contrast to the rough sports of the Clary's Grove boys, other villagers enjoyed social events of a milder nature. Clarke recorded: "I attended an old fashioned *Kentucky* barbecue last week . . . where they had feasting and drinking in the woods, the people behaved very well. There were many candidates present and each one made a stump speech. . . . I have an invitation to a wedding next thursday and expect to have a real succor wedding. It is to be in a log cabin with only one room, we shall probably stay all night as the custome is in this country, and the probability is, the floor will be the common bedstead of us all."

This custom of all sleeping together on the floor was necessitated by the size of the houses and the distance that people had to travel to social functions. Peck said of it: "On the arrival of travelers or visitors, the bed clothing is shared with them, being spread on the puncheon floor, that the feet may project towards the fire. . . . All the family, of both sexes, with all the strangers who arrive, often lodge in the same room. In that case, the under garments are never taken off, and no consciousness of impropriety or indelicacy of feeling is manifested. A few pins, stuck in the wall of the cabin, display the dresses of the women and the hunting shirts of the men."

Dances, house-raisings, wolf hunts, militia musters, and camp meetings made life at New Salem far from dull. Clarke wrote that at the frequent quilting-bees each of the guests would "take his or her needle as the case may be for any man can quilt as well as the women." Guests came shortly after breakfast, quilted until about two o'clock, then had a "good set down" until ready to go home. Once a circus came to Springfield, and several New Salem men, loading wives, children, neighbors, and food into farm wagon or buckboard, jounced twenty miles over the rutted road to see it. Impromptu foot-races and horse races provided amusement and thrills; and every year there were formal race meets in each county under the sponsorship of local jockey clubs. The horses for these events were imported from Kentucky and Tennessee "by gentlemen that do nothing else for a livelihood and some of them have as high as fifteen and twenty horses." The jockey clubs provided the purses, and betting was private.

A favorite pastime was shooting for a beef. Some one, wishing to make a little money, would announce that at a certain time and place a beef would be shot for. The word would spread, and settlers from miles around would gather at the appointed place. A subscription paper was then passed around stating, for example, that "Tom Watkins offers a beef worth twenty dollars at twenty-five cents a shot." The contestants subscribed their names with the number of shots they would take.

Jack Armstrong puts in four shots		*$1.00*
Royal Clary " " *eight* "		*2.00*
Jack Kelso " " *two* "		*.50*

Finally the twenty dollars would be made up.

Judges were then chosen, and each contestant made a target—usually it was a board with a cross in the center. Each man's target was placed in turn against a tree as he shot. The judges then took the boards and graded the shots, and the five best shots each won a part of the beef. The best one got the hide and tallow. The next best had his choice of the hindquarters. The third took the other hindquarter. The fourth got his choice of the forequarters, and the fifth took the remaining forequarter. The sixth got the lead in the tree against which the targets had been placed. An expert marksman, if he bought enough shots, could sometimes win the whole beef.

On the Fourth of July and during political campaigns, barbecues were held. Someone would donate a heifer, another a shoat; still others turkeys, chickens, pies, and loaves of bread. Long trenches were dug in which the fires were lighted a day or two before the event, so that a bed of red-hot coals would be ready for the cooks. The beef and pig were quartered and hung over the fire on long iron rods. Every few minutes, as the rods were turned, the cooks basted the meat with melted butter. After dinner came patriotic orations or political speeches, followed by athletic feats. T. G. Onstot recalled that they had a heavy old cannon, and the boys "nearly strained their gizzards out" to see which ones could shoulder it.

There was even a budding intellectuality in the place. James Rutledge is said to have had a library of twenty-five or thirty volumes. Dr. Allen was a graduate of Dartmouth. Jack Kelso, a lazy dreamer who knew where to catch the best fish, how best to snare small game, and who was an expert rifleman, was familiar with the works of Shakespeare and Burns and could quote long passages. The Reverend John M. Berry, who lived on Rock Creek but often preached at New Salem, John Camron, Dr. Regnier, and James Rutledge were fairly well educated. Rutledge organized a debating society in 1831. David Rutledge, his son, William F. Berry, son of John M. Berry and Lincoln's partner for a while, William G. Greene and his brother, L. M. Greene, and Harvey Ross, who carried the mail to and from New Salem, attended Illinois College at Jacksonville, about thirty miles away. In Clarke's opinion that institution was "doeing more for this country than any eastern man could expect," and its students "almost astonish the old folks when they come home."

The school at New Salem was taught by Mentor Graham, a serious, self-educated man in his early thirties who lived in a brick house about a mile west of town. He came to Sangamon County from Kentucky in 1828 and first taught school at the Baptist church on the Felix Greene farm about a mile southwest of New Salem. Referring to the subject of schoolteaching, Clarke informed his relatives back East that it was "good business worth from eighteen to twenty-five dollars pr. month clear. Schools are supported here different from what they are in N. England every one pays for the number he sends, there is no tax about it." A statement submitted by Graham to Jacob Bale, covering tuition for the latter's children from 1833 to 1840, shows that

Graham's subscription rates ranged from thirty to eighty-five cents a month for each pupil, evidently depending on the child's age. Five cents per pupil was his rate by the day.

New Salem enjoyed a relatively healthy site, but it was not immune to the malarial fever, typhoid, and ague with which the Sangamon country was afflicted. The latter disease was so common on the frontier that settlers hardly regarded it as a disease at all. "He ain't sick," they said, "he's only got the ager." In the early thirties there were cholera epidemics in the vicinity and in 1836 smallpox was prevalent. But settlers consoled themselves with the argument that these diseases occurred only in the summer months, and that there were no "lingering complaints like the consumption" with which so many Easterners were afflicted.

Pioneer remedies were a combination of domestic experience, superstition, and lore. Whisky, purgatives, bitters made from roots and barks, brimstone, sulphur, scrapings from pewter spoons, gunpowder and lard, and tobacco juice were tried for various complaints. Cayenne pepper in spirits on the outside, and whisky within, were good for stomach-ache. A piece of fat meat, well peppered and tied around the neck, was a common treatment for colds and sore throat. A bag of pounded slippery elm over the eye was supposed to draw out fever. Raw-potato poultice was tried for headache. The breaking out of eruptive diseases was hastened by doses of a concoction made from sheep dung known as "nanny tea." A seventh son could supposedly cure rash by blowing in children's mouths.

With many communities entirely dependent upon such homemade remedies or upon the prescriptions of local "yarb and root" doctors, New Salem was fortunate in having Dr. Allen as a resident. Young Dr. Regnier, stout, witty, eccentric, the son of a French physician, was a capable colleague of Allen's. Their judgment and experience proved invaluable to the community. Like most pioneer doctors, they worked under handicaps, for the self-reliant frontiersmen called the doctor only when home remedies had failed and drastic treatment was demanded. There was reason for their reluctance, for even educated doctors like Allen and Regnier used treatments of appalling severity. They "purged, bled, blistered, puked, and salivated." Twenty to 100 grains of calomel was a common dose. Pills were often as big as cherries. Wet sheets were wrapped around a sufferer to counteract fever. Severe types of ague were combatted by treatment designed to bring on the shakes. "Carry then your patient into the passage between the two cabins . . . and strip off all his clothes that he may lie naked in the cold air and upon a bare sacking—and then and there pour over and upon him successive buckets of cold spring water, and continue until he has a decided and *pretty powerful smart chance of a shake.*" [5]

Allen became as much interested in saving men's souls as in ministering to their bodies. He organized a temperance society in which he was assisted by John M. Berry. There was need for such an organization, for New Salem was a hard-drinking place. George Warburton, one of the town's first merchants, a thrifty, capable man when sober, was found face-down in the shallow water of the river after a drunken debauch, and Peter Lukins, another heavy drinker, also died after a spree. Few even of the better citizens were teetotalers, and Onstot recorded that Allen, in his temperance enterprise, "found his worst opponents among the church members, most of whom had their barrels of whiskey at home."

Much of this whisky was made in or near the town. Lincoln said that he worked the latter part of one winter "in a little still-house, up at the head of a hollow." In all grain-growing regions where transportation was difficult whisky was distilled on a wholesale scale. A horse could carry about four bushels of corn in the form of grain and the equivalent of twenty-four bushels in the form of liquor. Besides the economic motive, there

[5] Buley, "Pioneer Health and Medical Practice in the Old Northwest."

were other reasons for whisky-making. Whisky was a standard remedy and preventive of disease. Some people regarded alcohol as a necessity for persons engaged in strenuous work. While temperance agitation had made some headway and was destined to spread rapidly during the next decade, Allen was somewhat ahead of the times, for in the thirties the making and drinking of whisky were not generally condemned. The prevailing attitude toward liquor is illustrated by the fact that a man was dismissed from a Baptist church near New Salem for joining Dr. Allen's temperance society. At the same time another member was dismissed for drunkenness; whereupon a third member, rising excitedly to his feet and shaking a flask in his hand, shouted: "Brethering, it seems to me you are not sistenent [consistent] because you have turned out one man for taking the pledge and another for getting drunk. Now, brethering, how much of this critter have I got to drink to have good standing amongst you?" Camp meetings, funerals, weddings, and house-raisings were often enlivened by the unpredictable conduct of men deep in their cups.

Besides leading the temperance movement, Allen organized the first Sunday school in New Salem. A strict Sabbatarian, for years he refused to practice on Sunday. Finally he compromised by giving all his Sunday fees to the church. In his home all the Sunday food had to be cooked on Saturday.

The strongest religious sects in the New Salem neighborhood were the "Hardshell" Baptists, Cumberland Presbyterians, and Methodists. Strange new sects were continually forming, however, as the self-reliant pioneer—usually with untrained mind and faulty logic —exercised the prerogative of interpreting the Scriptures for himself. Clarke noted that, besides the denominations mentioned, many others existed "that deserve no name." Mentor Graham and Joshua Miller were leading Baptists. Onstot, Allen, Berry, and Camron were Presbyterians. Every year camp meetings were held at Concord and Rock Creek. The Rutledges, Onstots, and Berrys were enthusiastic "campers." So was James Pantier of Sand Ridge, an eccentric "faith doctor" noted for his ability to cure snake bites. "Uncle Jimmy," as the latter was called, sat on the front row and repeated the sermon after the preacher. If he disagreed with the doctrine expounded, he would shake his finger and exclaim: "Now, brother, that ain't so."

Peter Cartwright, the famous Methodist circuit rider, who lived at Pleasant Plains, ten miles from New Salem, often preached at these camp meetings, which were of the old-fashioned, emotional sort. Sometimes as the preacher warmed to his work and "swung clear," members of the congregation, overcome with hysteria, would be seized with the "jerks." Cartwright told of having seen 500 persons jerking at one time. "Usually

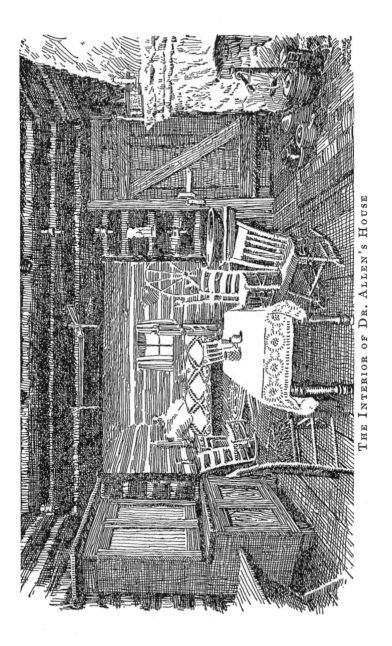

The Interior of Dr. Allen's House

persons taken with the jerks," wrote Onstot, "to get relief would rise up and dance, some would try to run away, but could not, some would resist, and on such the jerks were very severe." The women especially seemed prone to this hysteria. The first jerk would loosen bonnets, caps, and combs, "and so sudden would be the jerking of the head that their long loose hair would crack almost as loud as a waggoner's whip." Mrs. Robert Johnson, wife of the New Salem wheelwright, was particularly susceptible to the exhortation of the frontier preachers, being seized with the jerks almost every year.

There were smaller gatherings in the schoolhouse, in Dr. Allen's residence and other homes, where John Camron and John M. Berry preached and prayed. Onstot described "Old John Berry," a veteran of the War of 1812, as tall and well formed, "the noblest Roman of them all," who, "like Paul among the prophets stood head and shoulders above his brethren." Well versed in the doctrines of his faith, a leader in the Rock Creek lyceum and in the New Salem community life, Berry, said Onstot, "did as much to civilize and christianize the central part of Illinois as any living man." [6]

The ruffians of the neighborhood were a constant

[6] In 1849, after he had moved to Iowa, Berry published a book of *Lectures on the Covenants and the Right to Church Membership.* While disputatious and, like many religious books of that day, concerned primarily with doctrine, the lectures attest the author's ability.

tribulation to the religious element. When the Baptists immersed their converts in the Sangamon below the bluff, irreverent neighbors would throw in logs and dogs and otherwise disturb the ceremony.

There were also some freethinkers in the community who read Thomas Paine's *Age of Reason* and Constantin de Volney's *Ruins of Empire*, and who questioned the pronouncements of the preachers. According to Herndon, Lincoln belonged to this skeptical group.

The church members held little hope for them. Preachers threatened hell and damnation for those who had the gospel offered to them, but rejected it, and "could hold a sinner over the pit of brimstone till he could see himself hanging by a slender thread." Clarke observed that the Baptists "preach the hardest election doctring that I ever heard. They say they were created for Heaven (the church members) and such as die in their sins were created for Hell, or in other words, God made a part of mankind for eternal happiness and the ballance for endless misery. This is a kind of doctering I cant stand."

The Methodists and Baptists looked askance at preachers who had been college trained. Preachers of the old school suspected college men of having no religion in their hearts and knowing nothing about it except what they learned at school. Peter Cartwright rejoiced that he had not spent four years "rubbing his back against the walls of a college." Written sermons were taboo; and even preparation was frowned upon by some. A true preacher got his inspiration directly from the Lord as he spoke. Preachers often "made up in loud hallooing and violent action what they lacked in information."

Deeply concerned with creeds and the externals of religion, church members despaired not only of unbelievers and skeptics, but of those of different faiths as well. Julian Sturtevant, coming from Yale to teach at Illinois College, wrote: "In Illinois I met for the first time a divided Christian community, and was plunged without warning or preparation into a sea of sectarian rivalries, which was kept in constant agitation." Methodists and Baptists argued endlessly "about the way to heaven, whether it was by water or dry land," while both scorned the "high toned doctrines of Calvinism" and the "muddy waters of Campbellism." Cartwright told of a mother who, at one of his revivals, forcibly tore her daughters from the altar to prevent their becoming Methodists.

Yet religion was a potent force for good, and in some respects an intellectual stimulus. Sermons, poor as they often were, gave many people their only examples of creative mental work, while discussions of salvation, baptism, morals, and faith provided a sort of intellectual free-for-all.

Such was New Salem in its day; but its day was brief. Seven years after its birth its decline had already begun. In 1836 a last attempt was made to navigate the Sangamon when the steamboat *Utility* ascended the river above New Salem and then tied up at the dam. But the river fell rapidly, and there she stuck. All attempts to float her failed, and she was finally sold and dismantled. The most optimistic now admitted that New Salem had no future as a river town.

Meanwhile, as Springfield grew it restricted New Salem's trading area on the south and southeast. The growth of Athens narrowed it on the east. Beardstown, Chandlerville, and Jacksonville encroached upon it to the west and southwest. New Salem might have been compensated by increased trade with the growing settlements to the north; but trade expansion in that direction was prevented by the founding of Petersburg.

The original efforts of Lukins and Warburton to found a town in 1832 had not gone very far; but in 1836 John Taylor, of Springfield, took over the Petersburg project, had Lincoln resurvey the town, and promoted it vigorously. As settlers filled up the Sand Ridge and Indian Creek neighborhoods, Petersburg, rather than New Salem, became their trading-center. The removal of the post office from New Salem to Petersburg on May 30, 1836, foretold the former's doom.

Even before 1836 several of New Salem's first residents had moved away; after that an exodus took place. Dr. Regnier moved to Clary's Grove, and then to Petersburg. Whary, Burner, Waddell, Morris, Kelso pulled up stakes and tried their luck again farther west. Alexander Ferguson and Joshua Miller bought farms in the vicinity. In 1837 John McNeil, who had bought the Lincoln-Berry store when the Trent brothers failed, moved it to Petersburg. Dr. Allen, who had been an inactive partner of McNeil, followed soon afterward. Lincoln moved to Springfield. Hill sold the carding-machine and wool house to the Bales. As people moved away the Bales bought their land and eventually owned the entire village site.

By 1836 there were almost 4,000 people in the northern part of Sangamon County, and demand for the establishment of a separate county became more and more insistent. Petersburg was the prospective county seat. On January 15, 1837, Clarke wrote: "When I first came here there was but one store and two dwelling houses in Petersburg. There are now seven stores and the number increasing this has all ben don within the last year, the place would grow much faster if they could get carpenters to do the work. The town lots . . . were sold a little more than a year ago for ten to twenty dollars each, they now sell for fifty to one hundred and fifty, the reason of this is we are about to get a new county here and this place will undoubtedly be the county seat."

On February 15, 1839, the Legislature set Menard County off from Sangamon; and, as had been anticipated, Petersburg was made the county town. To New Salem this proved to be the final blow. Hill, Onstot, and its few remaining residents now deserted their old homes and established themselves in the more promising place. By 1840 New Salem had ceased to exist.

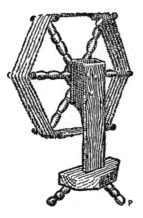

PART TWO

Lincoln at New Salem

ONE day in late April 1831 a crowd gathered on the river bank near the New Salem mill. They were watching four men working over a flatboat that had stranded on the dam. The men had tried to float the boat over the dam, but halfway across it had stuck. Now, with its bow raised in the air and shipping water at the stern, it threatened to sink.

One of the crew, a long, ungainly-looking individual, took charge. He was dressed in "a pair of blue jeans trowsers indefinitely rolled up, a cotton shirt, striped white and blue, . . . and a buckeye-chip hat for which a demand of twelve and a half cents would have been exorbitant." Under his direction the cargo in the stern was unloaded until the weight of the cargo in the bow caused the boat to right itself. The young man then went ashore, borrowed an auger at Onstot's cooper shop, bored a hole in the bow, and let the water run out. He then plugged the hole; and the boat, with lightened cargo, was eased over the dam.

Poling the flatboat over to the bank, the crew came ashore, where the onlookers congratulated them. The owner of the boat introduced himself as Denton Offutt. The others were John Hanks, John Johnston, and "Abe" Lincoln. The latter was the ungainly youth who had directed operations, and the villagers looked at him with interest. Well over six feet tall, lean and gangling, raw-boned and with coarsened hands, he was a typical youth of the American frontier. He had been born in Kentucky and had lived there seven years. Then he had gone with his parents to Indiana, where they had lived for fourteen years. About a year before they had moved to Macon County, Illinois. He was now twenty-two. Johnston was his stepbrother and Hanks was his cousin. Offutt had hired them to take the flatboat to New Orleans.

During their brief stay in New Salem, Offutt looked about appraisingly. He believed the place had possibilities, for the tide of immigration to the Sangamon country was rising steadily. He was convinced that the Sangamon could be navigated by steamboats, and loudly announced that he would build a boat with rollers to enable it to get over shoals, and with runners for use on ice. With Lincoln in charge, "By thunder, she would have to go!" He made arrangements to open a store on his return from New Orleans, and to take over the operation of the mill.

A strange combination, Offutt was enterprising and enthusiastic, but also boastful and vain. "He talked too much with his mouth." He was dreamy, impractical, too fond of drink. In a sense, however, he was the discoverer of Lincoln. "During this boat enterprise," as Lincoln later said, "he conceived a liking for Abraham, and believing he could turn him to account, he contracted with him to act as clerk for him on his return from New Orleans."

The remainder of the voyage was uneventful. At New Orleans cargo and boat were sold, and the crew returned by steamboat to St. Louis. From there Lincoln walked to New Salem, while Offutt stayed behind to purchase a stock of goods.

Lincoln reached New Salem in late July 1831. Shortly after his arrival, on August 1, an election took place. The polls were at John Camron's house. Here Lincoln voted, probably for the first time. His selections were Edward Coles for Congress, Edmund Greer and Bowling Green for justices of the peace, and Jack Armstrong and Henry Sinco for constables. The three last named were elected. Lincoln did not serve as clerk at this election, as has been often stated.[1] Throughout the day he loitered about the polls, talking, gossiping, and making acquaintances. By evening he had met most of the male inhabitants of the precinct.

At slack moments during the election he amused the bystanders with stories. Among others, he told of an old preacher in Indiana who was accustomed to appear before his congregation dressed in a coarse linen shirt and old-fashioned pantaloons with baggy legs and a flap in front, which buttoned tightly about his waist with a single button, thus making suspenders unnecessary. His shirt was also held together by a single button at the collar. Rising in his pulpit, he announced as his text: "I am the Christ, whom I shall represent today." About that time a small lizard ran up inside his baggy trousers. Continuing his discourse, the preacher slapped at the lizard, but without success. As it continued to ascend, the old man loosed the button on his pantaloons and, with a swinging kick, divested himself of them. But the lizard was now above the "equatorial line of waist band," exploring the small of his back. The sermon flowed steadily on, but in the midst of it the preacher tore open his collar button and with a sweep of his arm threw off his shirt. The congregation was dazed for an

---

[1] Herndon is authority for the statement that Lincoln served as clerk in this election. But the New Salem poll book, in the Illinois State Historical Library, shows that Mentor Graham and Abram S. Bergen were the clerks.

instant; but at length an old lady rose, stamped her foot, and shouted: "Well! If you represent Christ, I'm done with the Bible!" [2]

While waiting for Offutt, Lincoln lounged about town becoming better acquainted. He boarded at John Camron's. As days passed and Offutt did not come he picked up a little money by piloting a family, bound for Texas, down the Sangamon to Beardstown on a raft, and returned to New Salem on foot.

Offutt finally arrived, and the store was opened about September 1. It was the usual type of frontier store, its shelves covered with articles of every sort. Like other country stores, it served as a general meeting-place where all the questions of the day were discussed. William G. Greene, Jr., a youth of nineteen known familiarly as "Slicky Bill," whose parents lived about two miles southwest of town, was hired to assist Lincoln in the store and at the mill. Both men slept in the store. They became lifelong friends, and after Lincoln's election to the presidency he appointed Greene, a Democrat, and by that time a prosperous farmer and

[2] Rowan Herndon, one of those who listened to Lincoln, recounted this story years afterward to his cousin, William H. Herndon. It was evidently the kind of story that appealed to Lincoln's audience. It also tells something of the Lincoln of this period. Lincoln already had some of the knack of storytelling for which he was later famous. Here, however, he was telling stories merely for the amusement of the bystanders and to win their good will. He later used stories to illustrate a point or drive home an argument. This is but one instance of his growth between the New Salem days and the presidential period.

real-estate and railroad promoter, to be Collector of Internal Revenue at Peoria.

The store was situated on the bluff above the river near Bill Clary's grocery. Bill's brother, John, was the founder of Clary's Grove, and the grocery was the hang-out of the Clary's Grove boys when they came to town to trade, gossip, drink, or play. A reckless, roistering, fearless crowd, in individual and free-for-all fights they had settled the question of supremacy with the boys from other settlements. Rough and sometimes cruel, they were also generous and sympathetic. Not too respectful of law, they nevertheless had standards of right conduct which they observed themselves and to which they made others conform. They were typical American frontiersmen, with physical strength and courage as their ideals. Herndon said: "A stranger's introduction was likely to be the most unpleasant part of his acquaintance with them." Jack Armstrong was their leader.

Denton Offutt bragged continually of Lincoln's mental and physical might. He claimed that his clerk could outrun, throw, or whip any man in the community. The Clary's Grove boys were willing to concede his intellectual superiority. That was immaterial to them. But physical honors at New Salem had "to be won before they were worn." Soon Jack Armstrong challenged Lincoln to a wrestling-match.

Lincoln accepted, and the town turned out to see the fun. Bill Clary and Offutt laid a bet of ten dollars, while others wagered knives, trinkets, money, and drinks.

CLARY'S GROCERY

Armstrong was a formidable opponent, experienced, hard, and heavy-set. Lincoln stood six feet four inches and weighed 185 pounds. He had been a recognized champion in his former home. The two men circled warily, grappled and twisted, neither able to throw the other. Then Armstrong began to get the worst of it. Unwilling to see their leader go down, Armstrong's friends rushed in. Lincoln, thoroughly aroused, backed against Offutt's store, denounced them for their treachery, and offered to fight any or all of them singly. None accepted; and Armstrong and Lincoln finally shook hands and agreed to call the match a draw. From that time Lincoln had no better friends than Armstrong and his wife, Hannah.[3]

The match with Armstrong was an important event in Lincoln's life. It gave him the reputation for courage and strength that was so essential to success on the frontier, and convinced his associates that he "belonged." It gave him standing with the whole Greene-Armstrong-Clary-Watkins clan. While his physical prowess commanded their admiration and respect, his honesty and truthfulness soon won their confidence. During his remaining years in New Salem they followed and supported him in anything he did. Sometimes he acted as second in their fights; but whenever possible he persuaded antagonists to compose their differences. His jokes and anecdotes evoked roars of merriment.

[3] There are several versions of the Armstrong wrestling-match. The one given here follows that given by William Dean Howells in his biography of Lincoln. In the summer of 1860 Lincoln read a copy of Howells owned by Samuel C. Parks, and at Parks's request made corrections in the margin. He made no correction or comment concerning Howells's description of the wrestling-match.

Once he was second in a bloody fight in which his man was whipped. While the contestants were washing themselves in the river, the second of the victor, a small man somewhat the worse for drink, cried: "Abe, my man licked yours and I can lick you." Lincoln gravely accepted the challenge provided his opponent would chalk his outline on Lincoln and agree not to hit outside the lines.

The boys made him judge of many of their contests. It is said that he once refereed a cockfight in which one of the roosters belonged to Babb McNabb. Babb had bragged a great deal about the fighting qualities of his bird, and it was matched with a hardy veteran of the New Salem pit. Bets ran high. When the two roosters were thrown into the pit, McNabb's, seeing his battle-scarred opponent advancing upon him, turned tail and ran. At a safe distance he mounted a fence, proudly spread his feathers, and crowed lustily. Babb, paying over his wager to the owner of the victor, looked at his own bird. "Yes, you little cuss," said he, "you're great on dress parade, but not worth a damn in a fight." Years later, when General McClellan was exhausting the patience of Lincoln and the country by continually drilling and reviewing the Army of the Potomac but persistently refusing to fight, Lincoln remembered this incident and likened McClellan to Babb McNabb's rooster.

During the winter of 1831–2 Lincoln became a regular attendant at the meetings of the New Salem Debating Society. He had always aspired to be a good speaker. In Indiana he had sometimes stopped work to deliver extemporaneous addresses to stumps and cornstalks. In Macon County he had discomfited a visiting political candidate with an impromptu speech on the navigation of the Sangamon River. His efforts at New Salem were his first attempts at formal debate. R. B. Rutledge described his first appearance before the Society. "As he rose to speak, his tall form towered above the little assembly. Both hands were thrust down deep into the pockets of his pantaloons. A perceptible smile at once lit up the faces of the audience, for all anticipated the relation of some humorous story, but he opened up the discussion in splendid style, to the infinite astonishment of his friends. As he warmed to his subject, his hands would forsake his pockets, and would enforce his ideas by awkward gestures; but would very soon seek their resting place. He pursued the question with reason and argument so pithy and forcible that all were amazed. The president, at his fireside after the meeting, remarked to his wife that there was more than wit and fun in Abe's head; that he was already a fine speaker; that all he lacked was culture to enable him to reach the high destiny that he knew was in store for him."

Stimulated by the activities of the debating society, Lincoln determined to improve his education. In Kentucky he had been sent for short periods to "A B C schools," and in Indiana he had attended similar schools "by littles." But the aggregate of his schooling amounted to less than a year. As time passed, fewer people came to Offutt's store, and in the intervals Lincoln read. "After he was twentythree and had separated from his father," he stated in the autobiographical sketch that he wrote in 1860, "he studied English grammar, imperfectly of course, but so as to speak and write as well as he now does." This assertion places the beginning of his study of grammar in the spring of 1832, during his last months in Offutt's store.

According to New Salem tradition, he began to study grammar on the advice of Mentor Graham. Graham told him that John C. Vance, who lived on a farm to the north, owned a copy of Kirkham's *Grammar*, and Lincoln walked six or eight miles to borrow it. When a passage was obscure to him he went to Graham for help. He had Bill Greene and other friends ask questions from the book, while he recited answers and definitions. After he became President, Greene called on him in Washington, and, according to the story, he embarrassed Greene by introducing him to Seward as the man who taught him grammar. When Seward had left, Greene said: "Abe, what did you mean by telling Mr. Seward that I taught you grammar?

Lord knows I don't know any grammar myself, much less could I teach you." Lincoln replied: "Bill, don't you recollect when we stayed in Offutt's store at New Salem and you would hold the book and see if I could give the correct definitions and answers to the questions?" "Yes," said Greene, "but that was not teaching you grammar." "Well," responded Lincoln, "that was all the teaching of grammar I ever had."

Mathematics claimed his attention next. It held a lasting fascination for his analytical mind. In after years, while riding the circuit, he occupied his leisure by working out propositions in geometry and, according to his own statement, "nearly mastered the six books of Euclid." He read history at New Salem, and his interest in literature was stimulated by Jack Kelso, the village philosopher, who, though shy of work, was fond of hunting, fishing, and poetry. Kelso's wife took in boarders to supplement his earnings. Lincoln boarded with them for a while and listened eagerly while Kelso read or quoted Shakespeare and Burns. But he owed most to Graham. Always ready with help and encouragement, Graham was a constant stimulus. Rutledge said: "I know of my own knowledge that Graham did more than all others to educate Lincoln."

In the spring of 1832, "encouraged," as he said, "by his great popularity among his immediate neighbors," Lincoln determined to run for the State Legislature. On March 9 he announced his candidacy in a circular addressed to the voters of the county, which was published in the *Sangamo Journal*, and which Graham and McNeil helped him write.

The Illinois frontier seethed with politics. The national parties that emerged by the middle of the decade were just beginning to take shape, and political alignments were still factional or personal, with individual popularity and influential contacts as the requisites of success. Andrew Jackson was the hero of the frontier, and men were either Jackson or anti-Jackson, although many who supported Jackson personally did not agree with all his policies. These were known as "nominal Jackson men," as opposed to his "whole hog" supporters. Henry Clay was not far behind Jackson in popularity, and Lincoln made no secret of his preference for Clay. He had little to say on national issues, however, for, while these evoked a lively interest, local issues and local contests were of paramount importance to those whose votes he sought.[4]

Because of the absence of party organizations, formal nominations were unknown. A candidate, wishing to appear to run by popular demand, induced his friends to insert in the local paper an announcement

[4] The fact that local, state, and congressional elections took place in August and the presidential election in November also tended to give national issues and figures a secondary importance in the former contests.

that "Many Voters" would support him if he would run.
Other candidates sought the backing of influential politicians. Occasionally a man announced his candidacy by
a direct appeal to the voters, as Lincoln did.

Internal improvements, usury laws, and education
were dealt with in Lincoln's address. The two latter
subjects show the respective influence of McNeil and
Graham, but the remainder of the address, and especially its conclusion, is typically Lincolnian. With
respect to the first subject, he considered the deepening
and straightening of the Sangamon River the most practicable improvement for his own community. From
personal knowledge of the river he believed that, by cutting through some of its bends, digging a straight, shallow ditch of sufficient width through its lower course,
and damming the old channel, the river could be made
to cut a straighter and deeper channel that would not
clog with driftwood. This would be much cheaper than
building roads or railroads. He believed that a law
"fixing the limits of usury" could be passed "without
materially injuring any class of people." In cases of
extreme necessity, he said, means could always be found
to cheat the law! Education he believed to be the most
important subject that a people could consider. He held
that every man should have an education sufficient to
enable him to read the history of his own and other
countries, "by which he may duly appreciate the value

of our free institutions, . . . to say nothing of the advantages and satisfaction to be derived from all being able to read the Scriptures, and other works both of a religious and moral nature, for themselves."

THE MILLER-KELSO HOUSE

He concluded with the following frank statement of his own position: "Every man is said to have his peculiar ambition. Whether it be true or not, I can say, for one that I have no other so great as that of being truly esteemed of my fellow men, by rendering myself worthy of their esteem. How far I shall succeed in gratifying this ambition, is yet to be developed. I am young and unknown to many of you. I was born and have ever remained in the most humble walks of life. I have no wealthy or popular relations or friends to recommend me. My case is thrown exclusively upon the independent voters of the country, and, if elected they will have conferred a favor upon me, for which I shall be unremitting in my labors to compensate. But, if the good people in their wisdom shall see fit to keep me in the background, I have been too familiar with disappointments to be very much chagrined."

John G. Nicolay and John Hay, his wartime secretaries and biographers, who were probably more familiar with his later style than anyone else, observed that "this is almost precisely the style of his later years. The errors of grammar and construction which spring invariably from an effort to avoid redundancy of expression remained with him through life. He seemed to grudge the space required for necessary parts of speech. But his language was at twenty-two, as it was thirty years later, the simple and manly attire of his thought, with little attempt at ornament and none at disguise."

Lincoln's advocacy of the improvement of the Sangamon was well chosen and well timed. For months the possibility of navigating the river had been discussed; now it was to be demonstrated. In January 1832 Captain Vincent Bogue, of Springfield, announced that he was at Cincinnati, where he had chartered the small steamer *Talisman,* which he proposed to bring to Beardstown and with which he would ascend the Sangamon as soon as the ice went out. Navigation would mean cheaper goods, more accessible markets, constant contact with the outside world. The Sangamon country thrilled at the prospect. Merchants advertised the impending arrival of goods from the East. New settlers came; prospective towns were laid out; lots were sold, land values boomed.

Early in March, Bogue arrived in Beardstown. While at Cincinnati he had requested that several men with long-handled axes meet him and precede the *Talisman* to cut off overhanging limbs and clear snags from the stream. Accordingly, a boatload of men under the direction of Washington Iles, Thomas M. Neale, and Edmund D. Taylor made their way down the river, clearing the channel as they went. Lincoln was one of them.

Followed by a cheering crowd of men and boys, some mounted, others on foot, most of them seeing a steamboat for the first time, the *Talisman* puffed up the river. Passing New Salem, she finally tied up at Bogue's mill at Portland Landing, about five miles from Springfield. Her arrival was celebrated with a reception and dance at the courthouse to which Springfield society turned out in force. The event moved a local rhymester to write the following effusion, which was published in the *Journal:*

> . . . *Then what a debt of fame we owe*
> *To him who on our Sangamo*
> *First launched the Steamer's daring prow;*
> *And sailor-like went right ahead—*
> *Nor cared, nor feared the dangers great*
> *That on his devious course await— . . .*
> *Heigh, sirs, but I forgot to tell*
> *What great rejoicings here befell,*
> *Such stuffing—all the eggs in town*
> *I do believe were then crammed down,*
> *And the next morn Old Ned quite high,*
> *Had ris'n in price, and none to buy. . . .*
> *Jabez's good liquors went off slick,*
> *Some for the cash, but most on tick;*
> *The small beer poets made a show,*
> *And their small whistles loud did blow.*

The *Talisman* lay at the landing about a week. Then receding water forced her to start the return trip. Rowan Herndon, an experienced boatman, was engaged to pilot her to Beardstown, and upon his recommendation Lincoln was hired as his assistant. Making about four miles a day, the boat barely kept afloat as the river fell. At New Salem part of the dam had to be torn down to let her pass. Herndon and Lincoln brought her to Beardstown, however, received forty dollars apiece for their work, and walked back to New Salem.

Lincoln had scarcely arrived when there was another cause for excitement. For some time trouble had been brewing in northwestern Illinois between white settlers and Indians. In 1804 the Sauk and Fox tribe had ceded their lands in the Rock River Valley to the United States with the provision that they might remain on them as long as they were the property of the government. As squatters moved into the region there were arguments and minor outbreaks. In 1831 hostilities almost broke out, but the Indians were finally persuaded to move west of the Mississippi and to agree never to return without permission from the President of the United States or the Governor of Illinois. Nevertheless, in April 1832 Chief Black Hawk recrossed the river with three or four hundred braves. They came ostensibly to plant corn; but they were well mounted and well armed, and their coming spread terror along the Illinois frontier. A detachment of United States troops at Fort Armstrong on Rock Island watched their movements suspiciously, and an overt act by nervous militiamen precipitated hostilities.

Governor Reynolds immediately called for volunteers from the state militia to help repel the Indians. At that time all male white inhabitants between the ages of eighteen and forty-five were required to enroll in the militia and to provide themselves with "proper accoutrements." Refusal to enroll made one liable to punishment as a deserter. Those physically unfit or "conscientiously scrupulous of bearing arms" were exempt in peacetime on payment of seventy-five cents a year. The men chose their own officers.

Lincoln was of necessity a militiaman. When Governor Reynolds's messenger arrived at New Salem he was still clerking in Offutt's store. But the store was about to "wink out," and, having nothing better to do, Lincoln promptly volunteered for thirty days' service.

He was enrolled at Richland, near New Salem, on April 21, 1832. His company was composed chiefly of his friends and neighbors. The Clary's Grove boys constituted a large part of it. Lincoln was elected captain by an overwhelming majority.[5] In each of the two brief autobiographies that he later wrote he asserted that this honor gave him more satisfaction than any subsequent success in his life.

Jack Armstrong was first sergeant of the com-

[5] Lincoln's chief rival was William Kirkpatrick. It has been said that Lincoln once worked for him, that he cheated Lincoln out of part of his pay, and that Lincoln's friends determined to humiliate him by defeating him for captain. This story appears in W. D. Howells's *Life of Lincoln* and in other biographies. In correcting Parks's copy of Howells, Lincoln crossed out the passage telling of his having worked for Kirkpatrick, and wrote in the margin: " 'Wm. Kirkpatrick, I never worked for him.—L.' " It has also been claimed that Kirkpatrick resigned in disgust after his defeat; but the muster roll of the company shows that on April 10 he was promoted from the ranks.

pany. William F. Berry, soon to be Lincoln's partner in business, and Alexander Trent were corporals. In the ranks were Hugh Armstrong, David Pantier, George Warburton, John M. Rutledge, Bill Clary, Bill Greene, Royal Clary, Pleasant Armstrong, David Rutledge, and Isaac Guliher. A soldier of another command described Lincoln's company as "the hardest set of men he ever saw." William Cullen Bryant, who was traveling in Illinois in 1832, said that the volunteers "were a hard-looking set of men, unkempt and unshaved, wearing shirts of dark calico, and sometimes calico capotes." Some of the settlers whose farms they passed complained that they "made war on the pigs and chickens." For elected officers to exact obedience from such a group was no small task, and it is said that Lincoln's first command drew a retort to "go to the devil."

The volunteers assembled at Beardstown, where Lincoln's company was attached to the Fourth Regiment of Mounted Volunteers of the Brigade of Samuel Whiteside. They were mustered into state service on April 28. From Beardstown the brigade marched to Rock Island, where Lincoln's company was sworn into Federal service on May 9.

From Rock Island they marched along the Rock River to Dixon's Ferry, then south to Ottawa, where they were disbanded on May 27, their thirty days having expired. The march was uneventful. Lincoln saw no fighting. Once he was arrested and deprived of his sword for a day for disobeying an order prohibiting the discharge of firearms within fifty yards of camp. And when some of his men, without his knowledge, broke into the officers' quarters, stole their liquor, and got too drunk to march next day, Lincoln was again put under arrest and made to carry a wooden sword for two days. One day he saved the life of an old Indian who wandered into camp. The Indian had a letter from General Cass certifying that he was friendly to the whites; but this meant nothing to the frontier soldiers, to whom "the only good Indian was a dead one." They had enlisted to kill Indians, and saw no reason why they should not begin with this one. But Lincoln intervened. When some of the men denounced him as a coward he, "swarthy with resolution and rage," offered to disillusion them. The Clary's Grove boys supported him, as they always did in a pinch, and the others sullenly gave in.[6]

All of Lincoln's resourcefulness and adaptability were needed to supplement his scanty knowledge of military tactics. On one occasion, when he was leading his company across a field, twenty abreast, they came to a fence with a narrow gate. Unable to think of the proper command to "turn the company endwise," Lincoln

[6] Some authorities have considered this story improbable; but it is recorded in Howells, and was not contradicted by Lincoln when he made his corrections.

shouted: "Halt! This company will break ranks for two minutes and form again on the other side of that gate!" Herndon said that the movement was successfully executed.

In their leisure moments the volunteers sang, wrestled, raced, gambled, and played pranks upon one another. About the campfires Lincoln enhanced his reputation as a storyteller. He wrestled with champions from other companies, and at Beardstown met his match in Lorenzo D. Thompson.

When its term of enlistment expired, Captain Lincoln's company was mustered out of the service at Fort Johnston at Ottawa on May 27. On the same day Lincoln re-enlisted for twenty days as a private in the mounted company of Captain Elijah Iles. He was mustered into Iles's company by Second Lieutenant Robert Anderson of the Third U.S. Artillery, famous later as the commander of Fort Sumter.[7] Iles's command was made up of "generals, colonels, captains and distinguished men" from disbanded detachments. It was attached to a "spy battalion" or scouting detachment. While it was encamped near Ottawa, word came that the Indians had cut off the town of Galena, and it and other companies were immediately dispatched to the

[7] Albert Sidney Johnston, William S. Harney, Joseph E. Johnston, Zachary Taylor, and Jefferson Davis were other regular-army officers in the Black Hawk War.

rescue. Proceeding by forced marches, they reached the town without encountering the Indians and found the inhabitants frightened but unharmed.

When Lincoln's enlistment expired on June 16 he re-enlisted for another thirty days, this time in Jacob M. Early's company. Still he saw no fighting, but at Kellogg's Grove he helped bury five men who had been killed and scalped the day before. Their appearance made a lasting impression on him. Years later he recalled that "the red light of the morning sun was streaming upon them as they lay heads towards us on the ground. And every man had a round, red spot on top of his head, about as big as a dollar where the redskins had taken his scalp. It was frightful, but it was grotesque, and the red sunlight seemed to paint everything all over. I remember that one man had on buckskin breeches."

Lincoln was mustered out of the service at White River, Wisconsin, on July 10. His horse and that of his messmate, George Harrison, having been stolen the previous night, the two men made their way to Peoria, most of the way on foot. Harrison said: "I laughed at our fate, and he joked at it, and we all started off merrily. The generous men of our Company walked and rode by turns with us, and we fared about equal with the rest." John T. Stuart, Lincoln's future law partner, was one of those who accompanied them. At Peoria,

Lincoln and Harrison bought a canoe and paddled down the Illinois River to Havana. From there they trudged across country to New Salem.

In later years Lincoln treated his military career lightly. In 1848 in a speech in Congress in which he ridiculed the attempts of the Democrats to magnify the military record of Lewis Cass, their candidate for president, he said: "By the way, Mr. Speaker, did you know I am a military hero? Yes, sir; in the days of the Black Hawk War, I fought, bled, and came away. Speaking of General Cass' career, reminds me of my own. I was not at Stillman's defeat, but I was about as near it, as Cass was to Hull's surrender; and like him, I saw the place very soon afterwards. It is quite certain I did not break my sword, for I had none to break; but I bent a musket pretty badly on one occasion. If Cass broke his sword, the idea is, he broke it in de[s]peration; I bent the musket by accident. If Gen: Cass went in advance of me in picking huckleberries, I guess I surpassed him in charges upon the wild onions. If he saw any live, fighting indians, it was more than I did; but I had a good many bloody struggles with the musquitoes; and although I never fainted from loss of blood, I can truly say I was often hungry. Mr. Speaker, if I should ever conclude to doff whatever our democratic friends may suppose there is of black-cockade federalism about me, and thereupon they shall take me up as their candidate for the Presidency, I protest they shall not make fun of me, as they have of Gen: Cass, by attempting to write me into a military hero."

Yet in spite of Lincoln's bantering attitude toward his military service, Herndon believed that "he was rather proud of it after all."

The experience proved valuable to Lincoln in many ways. It provided him with a store of anecdotes. He learned to know something of soldiers and the soldier's life, the necessity for discipline and morale, the value and difficulties of leadership. He met men whose acquaintance would later be helpful to him—John T. Stuart, John J. Hardin, Joseph Gillespie, Edward D. Baker, and other rising young Illinois politicians. Just before they disbanded, the men of his mess agreed to support his candidacy for the Legislature.[8]

Lincoln arrived back in New Salem late in July, only two weeks before the election. He resumed his campaign at once, traveling from house to house, talking, making friends, telling anecdotes. As he talked to a farmer he would help him pitch his hay or cradle his wheat. At the crossroads he pitched horseshoes and wrestled with local champions.

He made few speeches; but at Pappsville, eleven

[8] April 16, 1852, Lincoln was granted forty acres of land for his service in the Black Hawk War. The land was located in Iowa, by his attorney, John P. Davies, of Dubuque. On April 22, 1856, he received an additional grant of 120 acres, which he located in Crawford County, Iowa, on December 27, 1859.

miles west of Springfield, a large crowd at an auction called on him to address them. As he rose to speak, a fight broke out in the audience. His friend, Rowan Herndon, was set upon by the friends of a man whom Herndon had recently whipped. The fight threatened to become general, but Lincoln strode through the crowd, grabbed the principal assailant by the neck and seat of the trousers, and threw him several feet. Hostilities stopped; whereupon Lincoln mounted a box and, according to A. Y. Ellis, a New Salem merchant for whom he worked for a time, gave the following terse speech. "Fellow Citizens," said he, "I presume you all know who I am—I am humble Abraham Lincoln. I have been solicited by many friends to become a candidate for the Legislature. My politics are short and sweet, like the old woman's dance. I am in favor of a national bank. I am in favor of the internal improvement system and a high protective tariff. These are my sentiments and political principles. If elected I shall be thankful; if not, it will be all the same."

Stephen T. Logan, a lawyer of Springfield who was later to be Lincoln's law partner, described him as he saw him for the first time at a political rally during this campaign. "He was a very tall and gawky and rough looking fellow then," said Logan, "his pantaloons didn't meet his shoes by six inches. But after he began speaking I became very much interested in him. He made a very sensible speech. It was the time when Benton was running his theory of a gold circulation. Lincoln was attacking Benton's theory and I thought did it very well. . . . The manner of Mr. Lincoln's speech then was very much the same as his speeches in after life—that is the same peculiar characteristics were apparent then, though of course in after years he evinced both more knowledge and experience. But he had then the same individuality that he kept through all his life. I knew nothing then about his avocation or calling at New Salem. The impression that I had at the time was that he was a sort of loafer down there. . . . But one thing we very soon learned was that he was immensely popular, though we found that out more at the next election than then. . . . In the election of 1832 he made a very considerable impression upon me as well as upon other people."

A. Y. Ellis told Herndon: "I well remember how he was dressed. He wore flax and tow linen pantaloons—I thought about five inches too short in the legs,—and frequently he had but one suspender, no vest or coat. He wore a calico shirt, such as he had in the Black Hawk War; coarse brogans, tan color; blue yarn socks, and straw hat, old style, without a band."

Lincoln was not elected in 1832. Sangamon County was entitled to four representatives, and there were thirteen candidates. Lincoln ran eighth with 657 votes.[9] As he later said, this was the only time that he was ever defeated on a direct vote of the people. But he was not discouraged, for in his own precinct he received 277 of the 300 votes cast, while the same precinct, in November, gave Jackson 185 votes to 70 for Clay. He had been in New Salem only a year, and his defeat was due to his being relatively unknown outside the New Salem community. From the campaign he derived an extensive acquaintance, valuable experience in public speaking, and increased confidence in himself. He began to realize his political possibilities, and he gained a zest for politics that endured to the end of his life.

The election over, Lincoln was out of a job. He pondered what he should do. He thought of becoming a blacksmith, but decided against it; thought of studying law, but was afraid to attempt it with his deficient education. "What he seemed to want," said Herndon, "was some lighter work, employment in a store or tavern

[9] At that time Sangamon County included the present counties of Sangamon and Menard, most of Logan, and part of Christian and Mason. The returns were as follows:

Edmund D. Taylor	1127	Abraham Lincoln	657
John T. Stuart	991	Thomas M. Neale	571
Achilles Morris	945	Richard Quinton	485
Peter Cartwright	815	Zachariah Peters	214
Archer G. Herndon	806	Edward Robinson	169
William Carpenter	774	William Kirkpatrick	44
John Dawson	717		

where he could meet the village celebrities, exchange views with strangers, discuss politics, horse races, cockfights, and narrate to listening loafers his striking and significant stories. In the communities where he had lived the village storekeeper held undisputed sway. He took the only newspaper, owned the only collection of books and half the property in the village; and in general was the social, and oftentimes the political head of the community. Naturally, therefore, the prominence the store gave the merchant attracted Lincoln. But there seemed no favorable opening for him—clerks in New Salem were not in demand just then."

Soon, however, an opportunity to become a merchant presented itself. New Salem had three general stores at that time—Hill's, Reuben Radford's, and one owned by Rowan Herndon and William F. Berry. The latter had acquired his interest from James Herndon, Rowan's brother, who, wishing to leave New Salem, sold out to Berry in the summer of 1832. In August or September, Rowan Herndon offered to sell out to Lincoln. At that time Lincoln was boarding with Herndon, who told his cousin, William H. Herndon: "I believed he was thoroughly honest, and that impression was so strong in me I accepted his note in payment of the whole. He had no money, but I would have advanced him still more had he asked for it." The Herndon brothers' store, where Lincoln and Berry first operated, was situated south of Main Street to the west of Peter Lukins's house.

In January 1833 Lincoln and Berry bought out Reuben Radford. He had incurred the ill will of the

THE LINCOLN-BERRY STORE

Clary's Grove boys, who smashed his windows, broke into his store, and demolished his goods. Radford was so angry and discouraged that he sold his business and what remained of his stock to William G. Greene, from whom he rented his store. The same day Berry and

Lincoln bought this stock from Greene, and shortly afterward moved into his store.

William F. Berry, though a son of the Reverend John M. Berry, was a confirmed drunkard. He devoted himself to the consumption of the firm's whisky, while Lincoln spent most of his time talking, joking, and reading books. Naturally, as Lincoln said, such a combination "did nothing but get deeper and deeper in debt."

At that time the question of how liquor should be sold was as much a problem as it is today. No license was required to sell it in quantities greater than a quart for consumption off the premises, and practically every general store sold it in that way. Only when it was sold by the drink, for consumption on the premises, was a license required, and only when the seller engaged in that sort of enterprise did he incur opprobrium. Places where liquor was sold by the drink were called "groceries."

Lincoln and Berry undoubtedly sold liquor in quantities larger than a quart; but there has long been controversy as to whether Lincoln sold it by the drink. Douglas in his debate with Lincoln at Ottawa, on August 21, 1858, claimed, half jokingly, that when he first became acquainted with Lincoln the latter was a "flourishing grocery-keeper in the town of Salem" and could "ruin more liquor than all the boys of the town together." Lincoln replied: "The Judge is woefully at fault about his friend Lincoln being a 'grocery keeper.' I don't know that it would be a great sin, if I had been; but he is mistaken. Lincoln never kept a grocery anywhere in the world." [1]

In view of this positive denial we may be sure that Lincoln never sold liquor by the drink. Yet on March 6, 1833, the County Commissioners Court of Sangamon County issued a "tavern license" permitting the firm of Lincoln and Berry to sell wines and spirituous liquors in quantities less than a quart, and beer, ale, and cider in quantities less than two gallons. The following entry appears in the records of the County Clerk:

> Ordered that William F. Berry in the name of Berry and Lincoln have license to keep a tavern in New Salem to continue 12 months from this date and that they pay one dollar in addition to Six dollars heretofore paid as per Treasurer's receipt, and that they be allowed the following rates (viz)

[1] Howells, in his biography of Lincoln, said: "It is supposed that it was at New Salem that Lincoln, while a 'clerk' in Offutt's store, first saw Stephen A. Douglas, and probably, the acquaintance was renewed during Lincoln's proprietorship of the store, which he afterwards bought in the same place." Upon reading this, Lincoln wrote in the margin: "Wholly wrong—I first saw Douglas at Vandalia, December 1834,—I never saw him at New Salem."

French Brandy per ½ pint	25
Peach " " "	18¾
Apple " " "	12
Holland Gin " "	18¾
Domestic Gin " "	12½
Wine " "	25
Rum " "	18¾
Whiskey " "	12½
Breakfast dinner Supper	25
Lodging per night	12½
Horse per night	25
Single feed	12½
Breakfast, dinner or Supper for	
Stage passengers	37¼

who gave bond as required by law.

It will be noted that the license was taken out by Berry. The bond required in connection with its issuance was signed with Lincoln's as well as Berry's name; but neither signature is in Lincoln's handwriting. Moreover, there is local tradition that sale of liquor by the drink was a primary cause of the dissolution of the Lincoln-Berry partnership. This is probably true; for in April 1833, a few weeks after the license was obtained, Lincoln disposed of his interest in the store to Berry.

At this time Lincoln's fortunes were at low ebb. In

debt and out of a job, he said in his autobiography that he was reduced to the elemental problem of securing bread to keep body and soul together. Many men in similar circumstances would have blamed the town for their failure and moved away, leaving their debts unpaid. But Lincoln remained. He believed that if he could succeed anywhere he could do so at New Salem. He had no intention of evading his obligations, and he wished to remain with his friends.

Except for the problem of debt he was not bad off, for with his strength and skill and reputation for honesty he had no trouble finding work. Travelers in Sangamon County in the early thirties remarked time and again about the scarcity of laborers and the good wages paid to them. Patrick Shirreff, a Scotsman, stated that "labor is scarce and highly remunerated. A good farming help obtains $120, an indifferent one $100 a year, with bed and board." He calculated that this was equivalent to eighty acres of land a year, and, in proportion to the cost of living and of land, about 800 times as much as English farm laborers received. C. J. F. Clarke pleaded with his family to send one of the boys to Illinois. "If he will learn house carpenters trade and come into this country," he wrote, "I will warrant him a rich man in a few years, finally tradesmen of all kinds are in great demand here and will be for many years, they get from two to five dollars pr.

day." Under such circumstances Lincoln could have had no difficulty in earning a living, and certainly there was little chance of his being in want.

But he was looking for a chance to become something more than a laborer; and on May 7, 1833, his ambition was gratified to some extent when he was appointed postmaster at New Salem, succeeding Samuel Hill. His explanation of his obtaining the position under President Jackson when he was "an avowed Clay man" was that the office was "too insignificant to make his politics an objection." He retained the position until the removal of the office to Petersburg on May 30, 1836.

According to one story, Lincoln's appointment was the result of a petition circulated by the New Salem women. Irked at the treatment accorded them by Hill, who neglected the distribution of mail while he sold liquor to the men, they petitioned the Post Office Department for his removal. Herndon did not know whether Lincoln solicited the appointment or whether it came to him without effort on his part. Upon appointment, Lincoln, like other postmasters, was required to furnish bond of $500. Nelson Alley and Alexander Trent were his bondsmen.

New Salem was on a mail route which ran from Springfield through Sangamon Town, Athens, New Salem, Havana, Lewistown, Jackson Grove, Canton,

and Knox Courthouse (Knoxville) to Warren Courthouse (Monmouth), a distance of about 125 miles. The
mail was scheduled to leave Springfield on Saturday at
four a.m. and to arrive at Warren Courthouse on Monday at eight p.m. On the return trip it left Warren
Courthouse at six a.m. on Tuesday and arrived in
Springfield at ten p.m. on Thursday, if on time. It was
carried on horseback by Harvey L. Ross, whose father,
Ossian Ross, of Havana, held the contract for the
route. After the stage line was established, it carried
the mail.[2]

Postal rates varied with the distance traversed and
the number of pages in a letter. A single sheet cost six
cents for the first 30 miles, ten cents for 30 to 80 miles,
twelve and a half cents for 80 to 150 miles, eighteen and
three-quarters cents for 150 to 400 miles, and twenty-
five cents for more than 400 miles. Two sheets cost
twice as much, three sheets three times as much, and so
on. Neither stamps nor envelopes were used.[3] Letters
were simply folded and sealed, and the postage charge

[2] By 1834 central Illinois was pretty well covered by mail
routes. Besides the New Salem route, six others ran from Springfield to various places. One went to Vandalia; another to St. Louis
via Jacksonville, Carrollton, and Alton; a third to St. Louis via
Carlinville and Edwardsville; a fourth to Peoria (where it joined
another going to Ottawa and Chicago); a fifth to Terre Haute;
and the sixth to Beardstown and Quincy.

[3] Stamps were introduced by the Post Office Department in
1847, but did not come into general use until 1855.

was written in the upper right-hand corner on the outside. Postage was paid by the person receiving the
letter.

The high rates on letters elicited numerous complaints. To conserve space people frequently covered
a sheet, then turned it sidewise and wrote across what
they had already written, sometimes following this by
writing obliquely across the page. Postmasters had
difficulty in determining the number of sheets in a folded
and sealed letter; and if the receiver questioned the rate
charged he could open the letter in the postmaster's
presence and have the error, if any, corrected.

As postmaster, Lincoln was exempt from militia
and jury duties, was permitted to send and receive
personal letters free, and to receive one newspaper daily
without charge. The law provided, however, that "if any
person shall frank any letter or letters, other than those
written by himself, or by his order, on the business of
the office, he shall, on conviction thereof, pay a fine of
ten dollars." A letter of September 17, 1835, from
Mathew S. Marsh to George M. Marsh, his brother,
throws light on Lincoln's conduct of his office. "The
Post Master (Mr. Lincoln)," wrote Marsh, "is very
careless about leaving his office open and unlocked during the day—half the time I go in and get my papers,
etc., without anyone being there as was the case yester-
day. The letter was only marked twenty-five and even

if he had been there and known it was double, he would not have charged me any more—luckily he is a very clever fellow and a particular friend of mine. If he is there when I carry this to the office—I will get him to 'Frank' it—. . . ." Lincoln was there, and did frank it, thereby making himself liable to a ten-dollar fine; for on the outside of the letter, in Lincoln's hand, is written: "Free, A. Lincoln, P.M. New Salem, Ill., Sept. 22."

A note from Lincoln to George Spears also reveals his indifference to postal regulations. "At your request," wrote Lincoln, "I send you a receipt for the postage on your paper. I am some what surprised at your request. I will however comply with it. The law requires News paper postage to be paid in advance and now that I have waited a full year you choose to wound my feelings by insinuating that unless you get a receipt I will probably make you pay it again."

The postal law required every postmaster to maintain an office "in which one or more persons shall attend on every day on which a mail shall arrive." By the time Lincoln became postmaster he had terminated his connection with the Lincoln-Berry store, and there is doubt as to whether his office was ever located there. Possibly it was for a while. Later it was in Hill's store.[4] Accord-

[4] Ross stated that Lincoln and Berry "kept the store in the same building with the post office." But Herndon says: "He made headquarters in Samuel Hill's store, and there the office may be said to have been located, as Hill himself was postmaster before Lincoln."

ing to Harvey Ross, Lincoln kept his receipts in an old blue sock, which he hid in a wooden chest beneath the counter.

Lincoln gave general satisfaction in his administration of the office. He was always anxious to please and accommodate. When he thought that someone was especially anxious to receive a letter, he would walk several miles, if necessary, to deliver it. Herndon recalled that "Mr. Lincoln used to tell me that when he had a call to go to the country to survey a piece of land, he placed inside his hat all the letters belonging to people in the neighborhood and distributed them along the way." The practice of carrying papers and letters in his hat became a habit with him.

As postmaster, Lincoln could read all the newspapers that came to New Salem. At this time he formed the habit of newspaper-reading, which he continued through life, and through which, in part, he learned to interpret public opinion. His position also enabled him to become acquainted with almost every settler in that part of the country and made more formidable his subsequent candidacies for the Legislature.

Financially the job was not much help to him. His remuneration depended upon the receipts of his office, which were small. More than a year after the New Salem office was discontinued, and after he had moved to Springfield, he turned over the balance of his receipts to

THE INTERIOR OF HILL'S STORE SHOWING
THE POST OFFICE

William Carpenter, the Springfield postmaster. Carpenter's account book contains the following entry under date of June 14, 1837: "For Cash recd of A. Lincoln late P.M. New Salem $248.63." [5] We do not

[5] Dr. Anson G. Henry, one of Lincoln's closest friends, and himself postmaster for a time at Sangamon Town, told Isaac N. Arnold that when the New Salem office was discontinued Lincoln had on hand a balance of some sixteen or eighteen dollars, which he brought with him when he moved to Springfield. Months passed before an agent of the Post Office Department called to collect this money. During the intervening time Lincoln had been financially

know how long this sum had been accumulating; but if it represented the receipts of the office for a year, Lincoln's commissions for that year would have totaled about seventy-five or eighty dollars.[6] If it represented the total receipts of the office for the three years of Lincoln's tenure, his commissions amounted to twenty-five or thirty dollars a year.

The *Sangamo Journal* of April 9, 1834, published the receipts of some of the Illinois post offices for 1833. The Jacksonville office took in $956. That at Springfield received $681. The Chicago office received $369; that at Beardstown $187; Peoria, $136; Pekin, $178;

---

hard-pressed, and Dr. Henry, who was present when the agent called, was afraid that Lincoln might not have the money. Henry told Arnold: "I was about to call him aside and loan him the money, when he asked the agent to be seated a moment, while he went over to his trunk at his boarding house, and returned with an old blue sock with a quantity of silver and copper coin tied up in it. Untying the sock, he poured the contents on the table and proceeded to count the coin, which consisted of such silver and copper pieces as the country-people were then in the habit of using in paying postage. On counting it up there was found the exact amount, to a cent, of the draft, and in the identical coin which had been received. He never used, under any circumstances, trust funds." This story and the entry in Carpenter's book may not be irreconcilable; but the entry makes the story doubtful.

[6] An Act of Congress of March 3, 1825, provided that postmasters should receive per quarter thirty per cent of the receipts up to $100. Then, on any sum over and above the first $100 and not exceeding $400, twenty-five per cent; on sums over the first $400 but not exceeding $2,400, eight per cent. They also kept fifty per cent of the receipts from newspapers, magazines, and pamphlets, while there was allowed "to postmasters whose compensation shall not exceed five hundred dollars in one quarter, two cents for every free letter delivered out of the office, excepting such as are for the postmaster himself."

Vandalia, $426. On the New Salem route the Havana office took in $54; Knoxville, $36; Lewistown, $130. No figures are given for the New Salem office, but in comparison with these figures the estimate of twenty-five or thirty dollars a year as Lincoln's remuneration seems more likely to be correct.

The position of postmaster was not confining, and Lincoln supplemented his commissions by doing all sorts of odd jobs, such as splitting rails, helping at the mill, harvesting, and tending store for Hill. In December 1834 he succeeded Dr. Allen as local agent for the *Sangamo Journal.* On election days he often made a dollar by serving as clerk, and sometimes returned the poll book to the courthouse in Springfield, for which service he was paid $2.50.

In the latter part of 1833 he secured employment as a deputy to John Calhoun, the county surveyor. Calhoun was one of the most prominent Jacksonian politicians in the county and Herndon says that Lincoln probably obtained the job through the recommendation of some Democrat. Knowing Calhoun's political affiliation, Lincoln hesitated to accept the job at first, but upon being assured that it would entail no political commitment he agreed to take it.[7]

[7] Calhoun was born in Boston, October 14, 1808. In 1821 he moved with his father to the Mohawk Valley. He attended Canajoharie Academy and studied law at Fort Plain. In 1830 he came to Springfield, where he resumed the study of law, teaching in a

Surveying in those days, when the country was rapidly filling with settlers and the division lines of farms were being run for the first time, when speculators were buying large tracts and laying off towns, and when miles of wagon road were being opened, was an important and responsible job. Lincoln knew nothing about it; but, borrowing books from Calhoun and enlisting the help of Mentor Graham, he went to work. Using Robert Gibson's *Theory and Practice of Surveying* and Flint's *Treatise on Geometry, Trigonometry and Rectangular Surveying* as texts, he studied day and night. Often he and Graham stayed awake until midnight, interrupting their calculations only when Mrs. Graham ordered them out for a fresh supply of wood

select school at the same time. He participated in the Black Hawk War, after which he was appointed county surveyor. He was in the Legislature from 1839 to 1841, was appointed clerk of the Sangamon Circuit Court in the latter year, was mayor of Springfield from 1849 to 1851, and an unsuccessful candidate for Congress, the State Senate, and the Democratic gubernatorial nomination. During Lincoln's first years in Springfield, Calhoun, at that time one of the strongest men in the Democratic party in the state, was an important factor in Lincoln's political development. He and Lincoln frequently engaged in impromptu street-corner discussions and sometimes in formal debate. He was a careful student of politics whom Lincoln considered a more formidable antagonist than Douglas. Milton Hay believed that Lincoln's discussions with him "habituated the sententious, precise, and guarded statement of political propositions for which Mr. Lincoln became so remarkable." Through Douglas's influence Calhoun was appointed surveyor-general of Kansas in 1854. In 1857 he was President of the Constitutional Convention at Lecompton. He died at St. Joseph, Mo., October 13, 1859.

for the fire. But he mastered the books, obtained a fifty-dollar horse on credit, procured a compass and chain, and by the end of the year was ready to start work.[8]

Calhoun assigned him to the northern part of the county—what is now Menard and the southern part of Mason County. For one of his early surveys, done for Russell Godby, he received two buckskins, which Hannah Armstrong "foxed" on his pants to protect them from briars. Ordinarily, however, he was paid according to the following scale, established by the Legislature on February 19, 1827:

For establishing each quarter sec-
tion of land $2.50
For establishing each half-quarter
section   2.00
For each town lot over ten, and not
exceeding forty   .37½
For each town lot over forty and not
exceeding one hundred   .25
For laying off land under a writ of
ad quod damnum   2.50

[8] Howells says that Lincoln, too poor to buy a complete outfit, used a grapevine instead of a chain, and Lincoln, in correcting Parks's copy, did not deny it. In his autobiography, however, Lincoln says that he "procured a compass and chain." Old surveyors claimed that a grapevine was as accurate as the old iron chains, whose links sometimes wore away to such an extent that they became several inches too long.

For traveling expenses he could charge two dollars a day.[9]

For several months things went well. With his commissions as postmaster, his fees as surveyor, and what he could make at odd jobs, Lincoln's earnings were better than they had been for some time. But in the spring of 1834 his good fortune was interrupted by his creditors.

While the speculative fever raged in 1832 and 1833, men ran up excessive debts, ventured on a shoestring, signed one another's notes promiscuously, discounted the future far beyond its possibilities. Lincoln succumbed like the rest, and had plunged heavily. His career in "high finance" began in August or September 1832 when he bought Rowan Herndon's interest in the Herndon-Berry store and gave Herndon his note.

On October 30, 1832, Lincoln and Nelson Alley signed a note for $104.87½, payable to Sheriff J. D. Henry, for the benefit of the creditors of Vincent Bogue, the owner of the cargo of the *Talisman*. The *Talisman*

[9] An Act of January 14, 1829, stated that it "shall be the duty of each county surveyor to provide himself with a well bound book, in which he shall carefully and legibly record and note down every survey made by him, giving therein the name of the person, the survey of whose land is so recorded, and describing as near as practicable, the metes and bounds of the land, and noting the date on which the survey was made: and such record shall be subject to the inspection of every person who may think himself interested." In the Sangamon County Recorder's Office there are two volumes of Surveyor's Records, beginning in 1841, but if Lincoln ever kept such a book it has not been found.

venture and other speculations had ruined Bogue, and
he fled the country. His creditors started attachment
proceedings, and in some manner Lincoln and Alley
became involved.

On January 4 or 5, 1833, Lincoln received about
$125 for his service in the Black Hawk War, and Berry
also got some money for his military service.[1] Instead
of applying this on their debts, the partners plunged
deeper than ever by buying Reuben Radford's stock
from William G. Greene. Radford, discouraged and
disgusted when the Clary's Grove boys smashed his
store, had sold his stock for $400 to Greene, from whom
he rented his store. Greene paid twenty-three dollars
cash and for the balance gave two notes for $188.50
each, secured by a mortgage on the store. Lincoln drew
and witnessed the mortgage, and that same day he and
Berry bought this stock from Greene, paying $265 cash,
assuming the payment of Greene's note to Radford and
throwing in a horse to boot. Thus Greene, on a rapid
turnover, made a profit of $242 and one horse. Berry
and Lincoln merged their old and new stocks and moved
into Greene's store.

On January 31, 1833, David Rutledge signed a

[1] As a captain Lincoln was paid according to the regular
army scale—$80 a month. Militia privates were paid $7.66 a month.
Each cavalryman was allowed forty cents a day for the use of his
horse and twenty-five cents a day for rations and forage when he
provided these himself. Each man also received a bounty of $14 for
enlisting.

bond agreeing to convey a half-lot to Alexander and Martin S. Trent, and Lincoln and Greene signed the bond as surety. Rutledge was a minor and had no title to the lot, but, on the frontier, circumstances such as these were often of little consequence.

In April 1833 Lincoln signed a note payable to Eli C. Blankenship, a merchant in Springfield. Rowan Herndon endorsed it, and on April 29 Berry executed a mortgage for $250 on the first Lincoln-Berry store (formerly the Herndon brothers' store) to secure it. It was at this time that Lincoln, and Berry dissolved their partnership, and Lincoln probably executed this note to Blankenship to get money to pay his debt to Herndon. Blankenship demanded that Lincoln find someone to endorse his note, and Herndon, in order to obtain his money, agreed to do so. Berry, unable to pay cash for Lincoln's interest in the store, helped out to the extent of securing his note.

By the summer of 1833 Lincoln's financial chickens were coming home to roost. On August 10 Sheriff Henry, on behalf of James McCandless and H. Emmerson, wholesale merchants of Cincinnati to whom Bogue still owed money, sued Lincoln and Alley on their note for $104.87½. Six days later the Trent brothers brought suit against David Rutledge, Lincoln, and Greene on the conveyance bond that they had signed in

January. On September 13 judgment for the full
amount of the Bogue note was entered against Lincoln
and Alley in the Sangamon Circuit Court. Three days
later Rutledge, Lincoln, and Greene reached an ami-
cable settlement of the suit that the Trent brothers had
brought against them, and the court dismissed the suit,
each party paying half the costs. It was about this time
that the Trent brothers took over the Lincoln-Berry
store, and possibly the transfer of the store was the
means of settling the suit.

On October 19, 1833, Greene's notes to Radford,
which Berry and Lincoln had assumed and which were
secured by a mortgage on Greene's store, matured, and
Berry, Lincoln, and Greene signed a new note for $379.-
82, payable to Radford one day after date. The same
day Radford credited them with a payment of $125,
leaving a balance of $254.82.

March 17, 1834, Lincoln and Alley paid the judgment on the Bogue note. But in the meantime Lincoln,
when he began surveying in January 1834, had incurred
an additional debt of $57.86 by purchasing a horse on
credit from William Watkins. Thus he was now indebted
to Radford, Blankenship, and Watkins, to the total
amount of $562.68. Lincoln failed to pay Watkins, who
sued him and Berry—the latter having evidently gone
on Lincoln's note—before a justice of the peace and

obtained judgment. The defendants appealed to the Sangamon Circuit Court, where the judgment was upheld on April 26.

Meanwhile, Radford had made a partial assignment of his notes to Peter Van Bergen; and on April 7 Van Bergen, with Radford's consent, brought suit against Lincoln, Berry, and Greene in the Circuit Court for $500 and $50 damages. The sheriff was unable to serve Lincoln and Berry; but Greene was summoned, and on April 29 judgment for $254.82 and $18.42 damages was entered against him. Of this amount, $154 was owed to Van Bergen under the assignment and the remainder to Radford. A writ of *scire facias* was issued to Lincoln and Berry to show cause why they should not be made parties to the judgment. Berry was served with process on August 15 and Lincoln on the 20th.

On October 11 Berry turned over a horse to Radford at an agreed value of $35, and on the 19th paid the balance due Radford. A month later Lincoln and Berry were made parties to the judgment, which, by reason of Berry's payments, was reduced by order of the court to $154, all of which was owed to Van Bergen.

Lincoln and Berry were unable to pay either this or the Watkins judgment, and the sheriff levied upon their personal possessions, including Lincoln's horse, saddle, bridle, and surveying instruments. Deprived of these means of making a living, Lincoln would have been

ROMAINE PROCTOR

The Interior of the Lincoln-Berry Store

in a sorry state; but Bill Greene turned in his horse on the judgment (probably the same horse that he had received from Lincoln and Berry when they bought Radford's stock from him), and when Lincoln's belongings were sold on execution "Uncle Jimmy" Short bid them in without Lincoln's knowledge and returned them to him.

On January 10, 1835, Berry died, leaving Lincoln solely responsible for the debts of the partnership. After he became a practicing attorney Lincoln repaid Short and Greene in full. As late as 1848, according to Herndon, he was sending part of his salary as a congressman to his partner to be applied on his debts; but he had probably paid them off before that date. Years after this, when Lincoln was president, Short was in serious financial straits, and Lincoln reciprocated his earlier favor by appointing him to a position at Round Valley Indian Reservation in California at a salary of $1800 a year.[2]

On February 11, 1835, the State Legislature passed an act providing that county surveyors should

[2] By the time that Lincoln left New Salem in 1837 he had sufficiently recovered from his financial reverses to buy two pieces of land. On March 6, 1836, he entered a forty-seven acre tract on the north bank of the Sangamon River in Crane Creek Township. He was probably not the sole owner, for when he disposed of the tract to Gershom Jayne on May 9, 1837, he gave only a quit-claim deed. On March 24, 1836, Lincoln bought two lots in Springfield for $50. Within a little more than a year he sold both of them at a good profit.

henceforth be elected instead of appointed, with the first election to be held the following August. Calhoun, who was running for the state Senate, was not a candidate for surveyor, and Thomas M. Neale was elected to succeed him.[3] Lincoln continued as Neale's deputy, probably until he left New Salem in 1837, certainly until the latter part of 1836.[4]

There is ample evidence of Lincoln's skill as a surveyor. Disputants over land boundaries frequently submitted their controversies to him, confident of his honesty and competence. He surveyed the towns of New Boston,[5] Bath,[6] Albany,[7] and Huron,[8] and resurveyed

[3] Neale was born in Forquier County, Virginia, in 1796. He moved to Kentucky, where he studied law. Coming to Sangamon County, he became a justice of the peace, was an officer in the Black Hawk War, and a candidate for the State Legislature in 1832 and 1834. He was elected county surveyor three times and held the office at his death on August 7, 1840.

[4] In 1850 Lincoln wrote to Joseph Ledlie, asking him to survey certain parcels of land that Neale had bought and sold to see whether there was any land remaining that could be sold for the benefit of Neale's widow, who was in straitened circumstances. "If Mr. Ledlie will take an occasion to carefully make such a survey, and thus ascertain the truth," wrote Lincoln, "I will do as much for him, in the line of my profession, at his order. I am not expecting any compensation from Mrs. Neale."

[5] New Boston was situated on the Mississippi, at the mouth of Henderson Creek. It was outside of Lincoln's territory, and he was probably hired to survey it by Elijah Iles of Springfield, one of the proprietors, or by Peter Van Bergen, who was Iles's agent.

[6] In a speech at Bath on August 16, 1858, Lincoln recalled that twenty-two years ago "he had with his own hands staked out the first plat of this town of Bath, then a wooded wilderness." That was on November 1, 1836.

[7] Lincoln surveyed the town of Albany on January 16, 1836.

Petersburg on February 17, 1836. Roads that Lincoln surveyed are still in use, and the boundaries of many Menard and Mason County farms were run originally by him. All over the territory he made more friends as he worked. "Not only did his wit, kindliness, and knowledge attract people," observed Coleman Smoot, "but his strange clothes and uncouth awkwardness advertised him, the shortness of his trousers causing particular remark and amusement. Soon the name 'Abe Lincoln' was a household word."

In the spring of 1834 Lincoln decided to run for the Legislature again. Development of parties had proceeded further than in 1832; but the fact that there was no presidential contest in 1834 tended to subordinate national and partisan issues and make personal popularity a more important factor. Indeed, Lincoln received backing from both Whigs and Democrats. The latter, "purely out of personal regard for him," offered their support through Bowling Green, a justice of the

---

It was situated on Salt Creek, about five miles west of the present town of Lincoln.

8 Huron was surveyed on May 21, 1836. It was located at Miller's Ferry, the main crossing of the Sangamon between Springfield and Havana, and was to be the terminal point of a proposed Beardstown-Sangamon Canal. Among the proprietors were Stephen T. Logan, Gershom Jayne, John T. Stuart, Simeon Francis, Ninian W. Edwards, and Samuel H. Treat. Lincoln entered forty-seven acres of land in the vicinity. (See note 2.) The original plat of the town, drawn by Lincoln, is on exhibit at New Salem.

peace and local Democratic leader, who lived about a mile north of New Salem. Lincoln hesitated to accept their support at first, but after consultation with John T. Stuart, Whig leader in Springfield, agreed to do so. "In this," according to Stephen T. Logan, "he made no concession of principle whatever. He was as stiff as a man could be in his Whig doctrines." His name first appears on the list of candidates—which was published regularly in the *Sangamo Journal*—on April 19.

Stuart told John G. Nicolay that, while Lincoln ran by general consent, there were strong efforts on the part of some of the Jackson men to defeat him (Stuart) because they believed that he was planning to run for Congress later. "I remember we were out at Danley's on Clear Lake," said Stuart. "They had a shooting match there. The country people met to shoot for a beef. The candidates, as was the custom, were expected to pay for the beef—and we were there electioneering. Lincoln came to me and told me that the Jackson men had been to him and proposed that they would drop two of their men and take him up and vote for him, for the purpose of beating me. Lincoln acted fairly and honorably about it by coming and submitting the proposition to me. From my experience in the former race of '32 I had great confidence in my strength—perhaps too much—as I was a young man. But I told Lincoln to go and tell them that he would take their votes—that I would risk it—and I believe he did so. I and my friends, knowing their tactics, then concentrated our fight against one of their men—it was Quinton—and in this we beat Quinton and elected Lincoln and myself."

Since Lincoln ran by common consent, he issued no formal declaration of principles. He made some speeches, but for the most part campaigned quietly, talking to farmers whom he met on surveying trips and soliciting votes as he delivered mail. At Mechanicsburg he won admirers by jumping into a free-for-all fight and ending it. Rowan Herndon, who had moved to Island Grove, remembered that during this campaign Lincoln "came to my house during harvest. There were some thirty men in the field. He got his dinner, and went out in the field where the men were at work. I gave him an introduction, and the boys said that they could not vote for a man unless he could make a hand. 'Well, boys,' said he, 'if that is all, I am sure of your votes.' He took hold of the cradle, and led the way all the round with perfect ease. The boys were satisfied, and I don't think he lost a vote in the crowd." Dr. R. F. Barrett of Island Grove, seeing Lincoln, inquired: "Can't the party raise any better material than that?" But after hearing him speak he declared that Lincoln amazed him, that "he knew more than all the other candidates put together."

On election day, August 4, Lincoln was elected easily, polling the second highest number of votes.[9]

During the legislative campaign John T. Stuart, in a private conversation, encouraged Lincoln to study law. His mind had always had a legal bent. Back in Indiana he had borrowed a copy of the *Revised Statutes of Indiana* and read it with care. In 1832 he had thought of studying law, but hesitated to attempt it. His interest continued, however, and in 1833 he bought a book of legal forms, with the aid of which he drew up mortgages, deeds, and other legal instruments for his friends, whom he never charged for these services.[1] He had even argued minor cases before Squire Bowling Green.

Green had his own methods as a judge. Although he was only forty-four, he weighed over 250 pounds and, from his protuberant stomach, was known as "Pot." He loved to laugh, and as he presided over court,

[9] The official returns were as follows:

John Dawson	1390	Thomas M. Neale	514
Abraham Lincoln	1376	Shadrick J. Campbell	192
William Carpenter	1170	James Shepherd	154
John T. Stuart	1164	James Baker	130
Richard Quinton	1038	John Durley	92
Andrew McCormick	694	William Kendall	42
William Alvey	613	Total	8569

[1] On January 31, 1833, he drew the bond by which David Rutledge agreed to convey a lot to Alexander and Martin S. Trent. *The Collected Works of Abraham Lincoln*, Roy P. Basler, ed., I, 16–17. He drafted the mortgage given by Greene to Radford on January 15, 1833. *Ibid.*, 14–15. On August 22, 1836, he wrote the will of Joshua Short. *Ibid.*, 51.

clad only in a shirt and trousers held up "by one linen suspender over the shoulder," Lincoln, pointing his long finger at him, would argue with great dignity and solemnity, then suddenly convulse him with a comical remark. In one case in which the ownership of a hog was in dispute between the Trent brothers and Jack Kelso the preponderance of evidence was on the side of the Trents. But Green awarded the hog to Kelso. "I know that shoat myself," said he. "I know it belongs to Kelso and that the plaintiffs and their witnesses lied." Green was very hospitable and often entertained Lincoln at his home. On such occasions Lincoln browsed through Green's scanty library and read such lawbooks as he owned.

After the election, acting upon Stuart's advice, Lincoln decided to study law with the idea of entering it as a profession. He borrowed books from Stuart, took them home with him, "and went at it in good earnest," studying alone, and, as he said in his autobiography, still mixing in the surveying "to pay board and clothing bills." At an auction in Springfield he bought a copy of Blackstone's *Commentaries*.[2] H. E. Dummer, Stuart's law partner from 1833 to 1837, reported that "Lincoln used to come to our office—Stuart's and mine—in

[2] It has been said that Lincoln discovered a copy of Blackstone at the bottom of a barrel of junk that he bought from a needy traveler simply to help him out. Howells says that Lincoln bought the book at an auction in Springfield and Lincoln let the statement go unchanged when he corrected the book.

Springfield from New Salem and borrow law books. Sometimes he walked, but generally rode. He was the most uncouth looking young man I ever saw. He seemed to have but little to say; seemed to feel timid, with a tinge of sadness visible in the countenance, but when he did talk all this disappeared for the time and he demonstrated that he was both strong and acute. He surprised us more and more at every visit."

Herndon said: "On the road to and from Springfield he would read and recite from the book he carried open in his hand, and claimed to have mastered forty pages of Blackstone during the first day after his return from Stuart's office. At New Salem he frequently sat barefooted under the shade of a tree near the store, poring over a volume of Chitty or Blackstone, sometimes lying on his back, putting his feet up the tree."

As Lincoln applied himself to books and worked less with his hands, some of his New Salem friends, unable to understand his ambition, accused him of laziness. Russell Godby, seeing him stretched out on a woodpile with a book before him, asked what he was reading. "I am not reading," replied Lincoln, "I am studying law." "Law," exclaimed Godby, "Good God A'mighty!" and walked on.

In November Lincoln interrupted his studies to prepare for the session of the Legislature. Borrowing $200 from Coleman Smoot for clothes, traveling expenses, and the payment of his most pressing debts, he was ready to leave for Vandalia, the state capital. Before his departure a meeting of citizens of Sangamon County, held at the courthouse in Springfield on November 22, 1834, elected him and ten others delegates to a State Education Convention to be held at Vandalia on December 5.

Lincoln traveled to Vandalia by stage, arriving in time for the opening of the session on December 1.[8] Vandalia, in 1834, was far from prepossessing. Its hundred-odd buildings, mostly log cabins, housed a population of about 600. Visitors were accommodated in "the very large tavern house, called the Vandalia Inn"—it had a dining-room 40 x 20 and thirteen lodging-rooms—"and the extensive houses of Cols. Black, Blackwell, Remann and Leidig." The House met on the first floor and the Senate on the second floor of the dilapidated two-story brick State House erected by the citizens of the town in 1824. Two weekly newspapers, one Whig, the other Democratic, reported the political news.

The town was situated at the intersection of two important roads, the "National Road" from Washington to St. Louis—not yet improved this far west—and a road that ran from Shawneetown through Vandalia to

[8] Howells says that "Lincoln used to perform his journeys between New Salem and the seat of government on foot." In the margin, opposite this statement, Lincoln wrote: "No harm, if true; but in fact, not true. L."

Springfield and thence to the northwestern corner of the state. The Legislature, the State Supreme Court, and the Federal Court for the District of Illinois held their sessions at Vandalia. Executive officials, legislators, judges, prominent lawyers, capitalists, and lobbyists congregated there. Many men brought their wives and daughters, and rounds of parties and dances enlivened the sessions. Vandalia was the hub of the state, its social as well as its political capital.

As a new member Lincoln played a minor part in the Legislature's work. He was conscientious in attendance, missing few roll calls. He received a few unimportant committee assignments, and drafted and introduced a few bills. He saw skillful lobbyists in action and learned at first hand of the logrolling that goes on behind the scenes in legislative halls. Saying little, he observed closely and learned much. Occasionally he dropped into the Supreme or Federal courtroom and listened to the arguments. The salary of three dollars a day was a welcome addition to his income.

Among Lincoln's fellow members at this session were men of affairs with trained minds and experience in practical politics. In the Senate were Benjamin Bond, brother of Shadrach Bond, first governor of the state; Cyrus Edwards of the prominent and wealthy Edwards family; William Gatewood, first commissioner of the Gallatin saline; Thomas Mather, soon to be president of the State Bank; Adam W. Snyder, who died during his campaign for governor in 1842; John W. Vance, wealthy salt manufacturer from Vermilion County; and Dr. Conrad Will, member of the first State Constitutional Convention. In the House were Robert Blackwell, one of the first Illinois state printers; Nathaniel Buckmaster, sheriff of Madison County in territorial days; Newton Cloud, noted Morgan County preacher, later a member of the Board of Canal Commissioners; General William McHenry, for whom McHenry County was named; Thomas J. V. Owen, one of the first trustees of Chicago; and William Ross, founder of Pittsfield and a delegate to the Chicago Convention in 1860. With such younger members as Orlando B. Ficklin, Jesse K. Dubois, William Fithian, and John T. Stuart, Lincoln was to have important contacts in later life. At Vandalia in 1834 Lincoln first met Stephen A. Douglas, then a young lawyer, whom he pronounced "the least man" he had ever seen, and against whom he voted for State's Attorney for the First Judicial Circuit.

Much more important than his participation in legislative activities at this session were the acquaintances that he made. Here he saw wealth, education, breeding, charm—things relatively unknown to him. Indeed, to Lincoln, with his hitherto limited contacts, narrow horizon, and in some respects provincial point of view, his first term in the Legislature was a liberal education, more valuable than anything that he could learn from books. Small wonder that when the session ended, on February 13, 1835, he returned to New Salem with his ambition fired, and resumed his legal studies with such determination that his friends were concerned for his health.

And now, according to tradition, Lincoln, in his twenty-sixth year, had his first romance. So far he had had no serious affair of the heart. Toward women in general he was indifferent or shy. At New Salem his closest female friends had been older married women. Hannah Armstrong, Jack's wife, at whose home he was a frequent visitor, patched his shirts and trousers while he rocked the baby's cradle or amused the older children. Mrs. Bennett Abell and Mrs. Bowling Green befriended him.

In 1832 Lincoln boarded at the Rutledge tavern, where he became well acquainted with James Rutledge's daughter, Ann, a pretty, unaffected, lovable girl of nineteen with blue eyes and auburn hair. She was betrothed to John McNeil, a thrifty young man from New York state who came to New Salem in 1829 and formed a partnership with Samuel Hill. With his share of the profits from the Hill-McNeil store he accumulated considerable property.

Meanwhile, he fell in love with Ann and became engaged to her. It is said that Hill was also in love with her, and that jealousy was a cause of the dissolution of the Hill-McNeil partnership. One day, quite unexpectedly, McNeil told Ann that he must leave New Salem temporarily. Before leaving he confided to her the story of his life. His real name was MacNamar, and he had left home and come west to seek his fortune, assuming the name McNeil to prevent his relatives, who were poor, from finding him until he could establish himself. Now that he was comfortably fixed, he intended to return to his parents, provide for their support, and then return and marry Ann. Before his departure he bought a forty-acre farm about seven miles north of New Salem on Sand Ridge, and to this farm the Rutledge family moved soon after his departure.

In Ohio, MacNamar was stricken with fever and for a month was seriously ill, part of the time unconscious. Finally he recovered and continued his journey. Arriving home, he found his father mortally sick; and after several months the old man died. Several more months were required to settle the family affairs. He wrote to Ann, explaining the delay, and she replied; but with the prolongation of his absence each exchange of letters became more formal. Finally the correspondence ceased.

Meanwhile, in New Salem gossip circulated. Mac-Namar's long absence, his assumption of a false name, the improbability of his story, convinced many people that he had been insincere with Ann.

During MacNamar's absence, according to the legend, Lincoln fell in love with Ann. But MacNamar was his friend, and he kept his feelings secret. As time passed, however, and MacNamar seemed to have left for good, Lincoln courted Ann. By that time the Rutledges had moved to Sand Ridge, so the courtship, if it took place at all, occurred there and not at New Salem. Sometimes when Lincoln went to visit Ann he stayed all night at the neighboring farm of "Uncle Jimmy" Short. Eventually Abe and Ann became engaged. They planned that she should spend a year at the Female Academy at Jacksonville while he continued his law studies and earned a little money. Then they would be married.

But in the summer of 1835 Ann became ill. Unable to eat or sleep, racked with fever, she became weak and emaciated, growing steadily worse. Despite all that could be done, it was evident that she would die. At first Lincoln was not allowed to see her for fear the excitement would be harmful; but when her condition became hopeless he was admitted to her room. "The meeting was quite as much as either could bear," said Herndon, "and more than Lincoln, with all his coolness and philosophy, could endure. The voice, the face, the features of her; the love, sympathy and interview fastened themselves on his heart and soul forever." About two weeks later, on August 25, 1835, Ann died.[4]

Lincoln was distraught. For days he could not eat or sleep. His face was haggard with mental agony. Ann's brother said: "The effect upon Mr. Lincoln's mind was terrible. He became plunged in despair, and many of his friends feared that reason would desert her throne. His extraordinary emotions were regarded as strong evidence of the existence of the tenderest relations between himself and the deceased." He complained that he could not bear the thought of "the snow and rain falling on her grave," and on stormy, gloomy days was closely watched for fear he would take his own life.

As his depression continued, he was persuaded to leave New Salem with its memories, and for a week or ten days he lived at Bowling Green's. There he pulled himself together. But for months, according to Herndon, he was subject to fits of deep melancholy, which recurred in less acute form throughout his life.

This story, discovered by William H. Herndon, first given to the public in one of his lectures, and elaborated in his biography of Lincoln, had immediate appeal. Popularized and sentimentalized by other writers, it did more than anything to create a general public interest in New Salem. In the minds of many people it

[4] She was buried originally in the old Concord Cemetery, north of Petersburg. In 1890 her remains were transferred to Oakland Cemetery, southwest of Petersburg.

came to be considered Lincoln's one true love—a mystic, guiding force throughout his life. Edgar Lee Masters expressed the feeling in the poem that is inscribed on Ann's tombstone.

"Out of me unworthy and unknown
  The vibrations of deathless music,
 'With malice toward none, with charity for all.'
  Out of me the forgiveness of millions toward millions,
  And the beneficent face of a nation
  Shining with justice and truth.
  I am Ann Rutledge who sleep beneath these weeds,
  Beloved in life of Abraham Lincoln,
  Wedded to him, not through union,
  But through separation.
  Bloom forever, O Republic,
  From the dust of my bosom!"

Under the careful scrutiny it has had, the story does not hold up; historians are practically unanimous in rejecting it as unproved.[5] Ann Rutledge was a real girl, to be sure, and Lincoln probably sorrowed at her death, as any person with his keen sympathies would do, especially in a small community where people live together closely and know one another well. But beyond that, the story has no basis in proved fact. Still it per-

[5] The best critical analysis of the Ann Rutledge story is in J. G. Randall's *Lincoln the President,* appendix to Volume II, pp. 321–42, where other studies of the alleged affair are also cited.

sists. It is as though people have an unexpressed, perhaps unconscious feeling that a life with so much sadness, so much tragedy as Lincoln's deserves to be enriched by such a romance.

A little more than a year after Ann's death Lincoln had a love affair with Mary Owens, an affair of sufficient seriousness to confirm the conclusion that he recovered quickly from his grief. Lincoln met Miss Owens, a goodlooking, well-dressed, sensible girl from Kentucky, in 1833, when she visited her sister, Mrs. Abell. In the autumn of 1836 Mrs. Abell returned her visit and proposed to Lincoln, banteringly perhaps, that on her return she would bring her sister with her if he would marry the girl. Lincoln accepted the proposition in the spirit in which it was made, and was pleased at the prospect of seeing Miss Owens again. But he was surprised when she did return with her sister. Since he first saw her she had grown stout and lost much of her comeliness; to Lincoln she did not seem nearly so attractive as she had been before. Nevertheless, he resolved to go through with it. They had some sort of indefinite understanding, and after Lincoln left New Salem to attend the Legislature in December 1836 several letters passed between them.

From Lincoln's letters it is evident that he was much perplexed, that he wanted to do the honorable thing, but that he was giving Miss Owens every oppor-

tunity to change her mind. Finally, in the fall of 1837
Lincoln made a definite proposal of marriage and was
rejected, much to his surprise and chagrin. He later
wrote, half jokingly, to Mrs. Orville H. Browning: "My
vanity was deeply wounded by the reflection, that I had
so long been too stupid to discover her intentions, and
at the same time never doubting that I understood
them perfectly; and also, that she whom I had taught
myself to believe no body else would have, had actually
rejected me with all my fancied greatness; and to cap
the whole, I then for the first time, began to suspect that
I was really a little in love with her." [6]

In a correspondence with Herndon, who investi-
gated the whole affair in 1866, Miss Owens, who had in
the meantime married a Mr. Vineyard and moved to
Weston, Missouri, explained that she rejected Lincoln
because he was "deficient in those little links which make
up the chain of a woman's happiness." Brought up in a
masculine environment, his social training had been
crude compared to hers. He neglected the little cour-
tesies and attentions that she deemed desirable in a hus-
band. She mentioned, for example, his allowing Mrs.
Bowling Green to carry her baby up a steep hill without

[6] It should be noted that, as Orville H. Browning explained
to Isaac N. Arnold, this letter to Mrs. Browning "was written in
the confidence of friendship, with no purpose, or expectation, that
it would become public. . . . Neither Mrs. Browning nor myself
ever knew from him who the lady referred to in the letter was."
See the *Abraham Lincoln Association Bulletin,* Number 25.

thinking to offer his help. She also told of his escorting her to "Uncle Billy" Greene's in company with other young folks. In crossing a rather treacherous branch the other men helped their partners across, but Lincoln, riding ahead, left her to shift for herself. When she chided him he laughingly replied, she supposed by way of compliment, that he knew that she was smart enough to take care of herself.

In the summer of 1836 Lincoln became a candidate for re-election to the Legislature. His campaign was similar to his previous ones. On June 13 he announced his views in the following letter to the editor of the *Sangamo Journal:* "In your paper of last Saturday, I see a communication over the signature of 'Many Voters,' in which the candidates . . . are called upon to 'show their hands.' Agreed. Here's mine!

"I go for all sharing the privileges of the government, who assist in bearing its burdens. Consequently I go for admitting all whites to the right of suffrage, who pay taxes or bear arms (by no means excluding females).

"If elected, I shall consider the whole people of Sangamon my constituents, as well those that oppose me as those that support me.

"While acting as their representative, I shall be governed by their will, on all subjects upon which I have the means of knowing what their will is; and upon all others, I shall do what my own judgment teaches me will best advance their interests. Whether elected or not, I go for distributing the proceeds of the sales of the public lands to the several states, to enable our state, in common with others, to dig canals and construct rail roads, without borrowing money and paying the interest on it.

"If alive on the first Monday in November, I shall vote for Hugh L. White for President."

During the week following the appearance of this announcement Colonel Robert Allen, a Democrat, campaigning at New Salem while Lincoln was away, stated publicly that he was in possession of facts that, if generally known, would destroy Lincoln's chances of election, but that out of regard for him he would not disclose them. Upon his return Lincoln wrote a forthright letter to Allen, declaring himself at a loss as to what Allen had in mind and demanding that for the sake of the public interest the facts in question be revealed. "That I once had the confidence of the people of Sangamon, is sufficiently evident," wrote Lincoln, "and if I have since done any thing, either by design or misadventure, which if known, would subject me to a forfeiture of that confidence, he that knows of that thing, and conceals it, is a traitor to his country's interest." Allen was silenced.

By this time Lincoln could take good care of himself on the stump. In the course of this campaign he made a speech in Springfield at the conclusion of which George Forquer, a prominent lawyer, arose and said that he was sorry, but "the young man would have to be taken down." Forquer had recently left the Whig Party and become a Democrat and had immediately been appointed Register of the Land Office. He had also built a new frame house, upon which he erected a lightning rod, the first one in town. After Forquer, with some show of superiority, had spoken at length, Lincoln replied. "Mr. Forquer commenced his speech," said Lincoln, "by announcing that the young man would have to be taken down. It is for you, fellow citizens, not for me to say whether I am up or down. The gentleman has seen fit to allude to my being a young man; but he forgets that I am older in years than I am in the tricks and trades of politicians. I desire to live, and I desire place and distinction; but I would rather die now than, like the gentleman, live to see the day that I would change my politics for an office worth three thousand dollars a year, and then feel compelled to erect a lightning rod to protect a guilty conscience from an offended God." Herndon records that the effect of this was "wonderful" and gave Forquer and his lightning rod a widespread notoriety. Forquer's house has been torn down long since, but even today Springfield residents remember their parents pointing out Forquer's lightning rod.

In the election, on August 1, Lincoln polled the highest vote of all the Sangamon candidates.[7]

The legislative session of 1836–7, which convened on December 5, was momentous in the history of Illinois. At that session was enacted the famous "internal improvement scheme" that provided for the construction of a central railroad, a system of minor lines, deepening of rivers, building of canals, and appropriation of $200,000 to be divided among the counties not otherwise benefited. In this orgy the Sangamon delegation, known from their stature as the "Long Nine," stuck together with a single purpose, skillfully casting their ballots for this and that project in return for promises of votes for the location of the state capital at Springfield. In this orgy of logrolling Lincoln took the lead, and it was largely owing to his efforts that on February 28, 1837, when the matter came to a vote, Springfield was chosen as the capital.

At this session Lincoln for the first time gave public expression to his views on slavery. During the early

[7] The vote was as follows:

Abraham Lincoln	1716	Richard Quinton	1137
William F. Elkin	1694	Thomas Winn	972
Ninian W. Edwards	1659	Aaron Vandiver	922
John Dawson	1641	Michael Mann	913
Daniel Stone	1438	George Power	905
Robert L. Wilson	1353	James Baker	101
Andrew McCormick	1306	John L. Thompson	38
John Calhoun	1278	Yancy	12
Jacob M. Early	1194	Total	18,279

thirties Northern Abolitionists, led by William Lloyd
Garrison, were driving Southerners to frenzy by their
incessant attacks on slavery. Several Southern state
legislatures passed resolutions denouncing such agitation and transmitted them to Northern legislatures,
some of which adopted resolutions sympathetic toward
the South. There was very little antislavery sentiment
in Illinois, and the Legislature passed a series of resolutions disapproving of abolition societies, affirming the
constitutional right of Southern states to permit slavery and declaring that the abolishment of slavery in the
district of Columbia by the Federal government, without the consent of the people of the District, would be
a manifest breach of faith. These resolutions were
adopted by a vote of seventy-seven to six, Lincoln vot-
ing nay.

Six weeks later he and Daniel Stone entered a protest upon the House *Journal*, explaining that their refusal to vote for the resolutions was due to their belief
"that the institution of slavery is founded on both in-
justice and bad policy; but that the promulgation of
abolition doctrines tends rather to increase than abate
its evils," that Congress had no power to interfere with
it in the states, but could abolish it in the District of
Columbia, although it should exercise that power only
at the request of the people of the District. Lincoln was
not aggressive in his stand, and was careful to disclaim

any sympathy for abolitionism. He went no further than his conscience demanded, and it is significant that his protest was not entered before his larger purpose of securing the state capital for Springfield had been achieved.

In this session Lincoln so impressed his colleagues with his qualities of leadership that in the following session he became the Whig candidate for speaker. Although defeated for that office, he was recognized throughout the session as the Whig floor leader.

On September 9, 1836, Lincoln had been granted a license to practice law, and on March 1, 1837, the Supreme Court granted him a certificate of admission to the bar. When the Legislature adjourned on March 6 he returned to New Salem. But the town held no promise for him. There was no chance there for a legal or a wider political career. Springfield, however, offered opportunities for both. Already Lincoln was well acquainted there, and his efforts in securing the removal of the capital had increased his popularity. John T. Stuart was willing to take him as his law partner. On April 15, 1837, Lincoln, astride a borrowed horse, with all his personal possessions in his saddlebags, moved to Springfield. Joshua Speed, a young merchant, learning that he did not have money enough to buy a bedstead, offered to share with him his double bed and large room above his store. Lincoln accepted gratefully. Slinging his saddlebags over his arm, he climbed the stairs, deposited the bags on the floor, and returned; and with his face beaming with a smile, remarked: "Well, Speed, I'm moved."

In his six years at New Salem Lincoln had gone far. He could justly take pride in his progress. Coming to the village like "a piece of floating driftwood," as he said, he had worked his way up to a position of leadership not only in New Salem but in the state as well. He was recognized as a skillful politician. He had made valuable friendships in the county and the state at large. He had learned to think straight and express himself with force and clarity. He had equipped himself to make a living with his brain instead of his hands.

To New Salem he owed much. His associations there were more varied than any he had known in Kentucky, Indiana, or his earlier home in Illinois. His advent there was a definite step forward—one that freed him from the retarding influence of his family and revealed to him the possibility of self-betterment.

The New Salem years left a lasting impress. To the end of his life the rural background of his early years colored his writings and speech. Many of the similes and metaphors that enrich his literary style smack of the countryside. The "twang of the crossroads" was in his anecdotes. Often in later life he illustrated his remarks with rural analogies drawn from his New Salem experiences.

In New Salem as well as in his former homes in Kentucky and Indiana, Lincoln lived in a Southern pioneer atmosphere. His contact with its people helped him understand the Southern temperament and point of view. He entered with zest into the theological discussions of the community and profited by the niceties of thought, the subtle distinctions, and finespun argument that they necessitated. Yet, while he enjoyed them as a mental exercise, and while he eventually attained to a deep faith, emotionally the bitterness of sectarian prejudice must have been repellent to him, and was probably a cause of his lasting reluctance to affiliate with any sect.

The New Salem environment, typical of that of the West in general, offered opportunities that Lincoln would not have had in an older community. Humble origin and lack of schooling were no handicaps, for they were common deficiencies. A newcomer had no difficulty in establishing himself, for no one had been there long, no propertied class had emerged, and social castes were unknown. Equality of opportunity was in large degree a fact, and democracy and nationalism were the political ideals.

Lincoln accepted these ideals and benefited by the

opportunities that the frontier afforded. But at the same time he avoided the frontier's weaknesses or, learning from experience, outgrew them. He became self-reliant without becoming boastful and without over-estimating himself; analytical and conservative rather than opportunistic and impulsive. He realized the value of law, and was respectful of form and tradition, in a region where men sometimes made their own law, where informality prevailed, and where people were concerned with the present and future rather than the past.

His support of Clay rather than Jackson, his defense of the old Indian in the Black Hawk War, his stand on slavery show that he was thinking for himself, and that here—as later in his opposition to the Mexican War and in the tolerant and forgiving spirit that he maintained toward the South in the prevailing bitterness of civil war—he dared stand against the crowd. His standards and ambitions transcended those of the community. At New Salem, as in later life, his individuality stands out. Yet while becoming a leader of his fellows, Lincoln never lost touch with them. He grew beyond his associates, but not away from them.

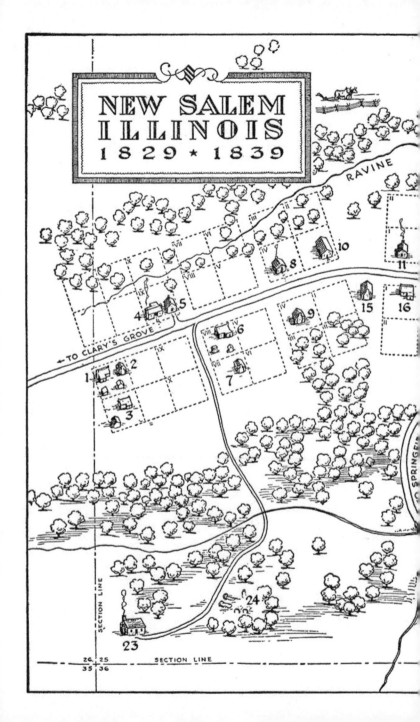

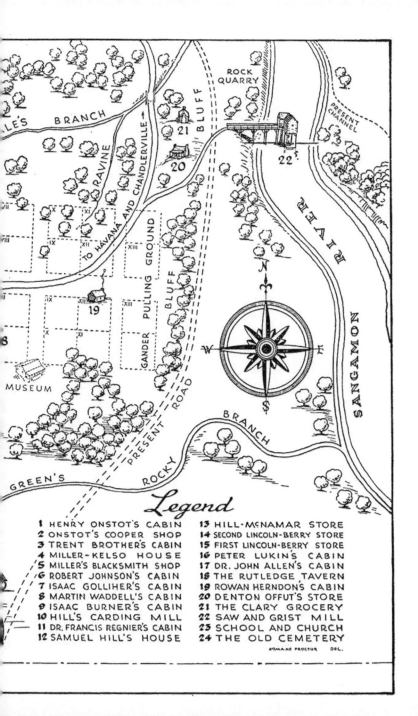

Legend

1 HENRY ONSTOT'S CABIN
2 ONSTOT'S COOPER SHOP
3 TRENT BROTHER'S CABIN
4 MILLER-KELSO HOUSE
5 MILLER'S BLACKSMITH SHOP
6 ROBERT JOHNSON'S CABIN
7 ISAAC GOLLIHER'S CABIN
8 MARTIN WADDELL'S CABIN
9 ISAAC BURNER'S CABIN
10 HILL'S CARDING MILL
11 DR. FRANCIS REGNIER'S CABIN
12 SAMUEL HILL'S HOUSE
13 HILL-McNAMAR STORE
14 SECOND LINCOLN-BERRY STORE
15 FIRST LINCOLN-BERRY STORE
16 PETER LUKIN'S CABIN
17 DR. JOHN ALLEN'S CABIN
18 THE RUTLEDGE TAVERN
19 ROWAN HERNDON'S CABIN
20 DENTON OFFUT'S STORE
21 THE CLARY GROCERY
22 SAW AND GRIST MILL
23 SCHOOL AND CHURCH
24 THE OLD CEMETERY

ROMAINE PROCTOR   DEL.

PART THREE

New Salem Restored

S ALEM, indeed, is desolate," observed a traveler along the road to Petersburg in 1847. "Once it was a busy, thriving place. It is (or was) situated upon a high bluff, overlooking the Sangamon river and the country for some distance around. What rollicking times were there some ten years ago? It is said that a horse race came off regularly every Saturday afternoon —a drinking spree followed, perhaps a fight or so, and at night those disposed took a turn at old sledge, or poker. But the glories of Salem have departed.—Most of those whilom engaged in the 'joust and tournament there,' have left the 'diggings.' Petersburg has been built up, on a pleasant site, a few miles below." In 1866 "one lone and solitary log hut" was all that remained. A few years later even that had gone. For more than sixty years the site was deserted.

But as New Salem moldered a Lincoln legend grew.

The place assumed a new importance as a factor in the making of the man.

Lincoln's contact with the New Salem people did not cease with his removal to Springfield and the village's demise. Many of those people moved to Petersburg, while others continued to live in Menard County. From 1839 to 1847 that county was included in the Eighth Judicial Circuit, and Lincoln, traveling that circuit, appeared in Petersburg every spring and fall when court convened. The list of his clients reads like a roster of old settlers. He was retained by Reason Shipley, Jacob Bale, John Purkepile, James Meadows, Isaac Cogdale, George Blane, Bluford Atterbury, William White, Jacob and Joshua Williams, John Taylor, John Tibbs, George Miller, Elihu Bone. David Rutledge, brother of Ann and one of Petersburg's first attorneys, opposed him in several cases.

In 1842, as attorney for Dr. Allen, he sued Samuel Hill for trespass *vi et armis* and got damages for $20 for his client. In 1845 Nancy Green, widow of his friend Bowling Green, retained him in a suit against his old teacher, Mentor Graham, on a promissory note for $112.23; and Graham, confessing judgment, paid the debt. In 1857 Hannah Armstrong, Jack's widow, appealed to him to defend her son, "Duff," who was on trial for murder at Beardstown. Lincoln did so, and Duff was acquitted.

After 1847, when Menard County was transferred from the Eighth Circuit, Lincoln turned over his practice there to his partner, William H. Herndon, and through Herndon kept in touch with his old friends. During political campaigns he spoke at Petersburg, and there had opportunity to see and talk to them. When he ran for Congress in 1846, Menard County gave him 456 votes to 336 for his opponent, Peter Cartwright.

But with the crystallization of the slavery issue the county became Democratic, although its vote was always close. In 1858, when Lincoln made his campaign against Douglas, the Democratic candidate for the State Legislature carried it 812 to 790. In 1860 it gave Douglas 1,035 votes for president against Lincoln's 962. By this time its population was more than double what it had been twenty years before, and the newcomers outnumbered the old residents.

During Lincoln's presidency, and after his death, as his greatness came to be appreciated, his New Salem acquaintances recalled with pride their earlier association with him. They never tired of talking about him, and every story found an eager audience. Gradually in Menard County a Lincoln legend grew, centering around the site of old New Salem and permeating all that countryside.

Naturally these simple folk were tremendously impressed at having known a man who had attained fame such as Lincoln's. As they recalled the days when they had known him, not only were their memories stimulated, their imaginations were quickened. In the light of Lincoln's later accomplishments it was inevitable that they should make a hero of him. They flattered themselves that even in the New Salem days they had recognized in him a man of genius and destiny. Their stories had a naïve boastfulness and self-complacency —often it was "me and Lincoln."

They told tales of his amazing strength. James Short recalled seeing him lift "1000 pounds of shot by main strength." Rowan Herndon testified that he was "by fare the stoutest man that i ever took hold of i was a mear child in his hands and i Considered myself as good a man as there was in the Country until he come about i saw him Lift Between 1000 and 1300 lbs of Rock waid in a Box." "I have seen him frequently take a barrel of whiskey by the chimes," said R. B. Rutledge, "and lift it up to his face as if to drink from the bung hole." Bill Greene told of having bet a man a fur hat that Lincoln could lift a whisky barrel and drink from the bung, and of winning when Lincoln rolled the barrel on his knees and did so, then spat the liquor out.

As a worker he was unexcelled. "My, how he could chop!" said one man. "His ax would flash and bite into a sugar tree or sycamore, and down it would come. If you heard him fellin' trees in a clearin', you would say

there were three men at work the way the trees fell."
James Short declared: "He was the best hand at husk-
ing corn on the stalk I ever saw. I used to consider myself very good; but he would gather two loads to my
one."

People recollected his honesty and kindness. In
making change for a woman, while working in Offutt's
store, he took out six and a quarter cents too much,
and at closing time, discovering his error, walked six
miles to return the money. On another occasion, after
weighing out some tea, he found a four-ounce weight on
the scales, and again walked several miles to correct his
mistake. Such acts as these won him the nickname "Honest Abe."

He helped a barefoot boy split rails to get money
to buy a pair of shoes. He offered the horse on which
he was riding to Dr. Chandler of Chandlerville to help
him reach the Land Office ahead of a "land shark" who
wanted his farm. In resurveying the town of Petersburg
he ran the lines out of plumb to prevent the house of
Jemima Elmore, widow of a comrade in the Black Hawk
War, from being in the street.

When a loafer offended his women customers by
persistent swearing he took him out and thrashed him.
Sometimes he restrained his rash associates from an
especially cruel prank. He stopped them from rolling
an old drunkard down the bluff in a barrel, although

the victim had agreed to let them do it for a drink. He dissuaded Jack Armstrong from thrashing a stranger who refused to be bullied.

"In the rôle of story telling I never knew his equal," T. G. Onstot testified. "His power of mimicry was very great. He could perfectly mimic a Dutchman, Irishman or Negro. . . . I have heard men say that they had laughed at his stories until they had almost shaken their ribs loose. I heard cases where men have been suffering for years with some bodily ailments and could get no relief but who have gone a couple of evenings and listened to Lincoln and laughed their ailments away and became hale and hearty men, giving Lincoln credit of being their healer."

They remembered his intensive application to his books; how he stretched out on the counter of the store with his head on a bolt of calico and an open book in his hands, how at night he heaped shavings on the fire in Onstot's cooper shop and read by the flames. He read until late at night and arose early to read more. He carried an open book before him as he sauntered down the street to his meals. Sometimes he was so abstracted and absorbed in thought that they had considered him "queer."

They marveled at his mental aptitude. He mastered surveying in six weeks, grammar in three. Mentor Graham told Herndon that in his forty-five years of teaching he had never seen anyone as quick and apt as Lincoln, that he was the "most studious, diligent, strait forward young man in the pursuit of a knowledge and literature than any among the five thousand I have taught in schools." Dr. Jason Duncan testified that Lincoln mastered Kirkham "in an astonishing manner."

The exact proportion of truth in these tales of miraculous achievement is of no great importance. What matters is that the people of Menard County were keeping alive the remembrance of Lincoln's residence among them. And fortunate it was that this should be the case, for the world at large, for several years after Lincoln's death, was only mildly interested in the New Salem period of his life. The campaign biographies of 1860 and 1864 contained little about it, and the first biographies written after 1865 were sketchy on that period. In popular conception Lincoln was the liberator of the slaves, the patient, kindly martyr to the cause of liberty and union. His ancestry and early environment were looked upon as handicaps, his rise and character as mysteries.

Early in Lincoln's administration his young secretaries, John G. Nicolay and John Hay, conceived the idea of writing a biography of him. They collected notes and documents and, after Lincoln's death, secured permission to use the manuscripts and letters that had come into the possession of Lincoln's son, Robert. They worked for more than twenty years and finally, in 1886, published part of their material in a series of articles in the *Century Magazine*. In 1890 their ten-volume *Abraham Lincoln: A History* was published.

Their book was really a history of the Civil War, and the Lincoln about whom they wrote was the war-time executive, the "mighty counselor whose patient courage and wisdom saved the life of the republic in its darkest hour." Their purpose was "to show his relations to the times in which he moved, the stupendous issues he controlled, the remarkable men by whom he was surrounded." They were less interested in and less familiar with his early life and naturally gave less attention to it.

In 1894, at the suggestion of Robert Lincoln, Nicolay and Hay published an edition of Lincoln's works, thus enabling people to read Lincoln's letters and speeches for themselves and to draw their own conclusions from them. These writings strikingly revealed Lincoln's character and individuality. They showed that many of the qualities that made him great were present early in his life, while others were of long development. They stimulated interest in his earlier years and led students to seek the explanation of him in his heredity and environment.

Meanwhile, William H. Herndon, Lincoln's law partner from 1844 until Lincoln's death, having worked along independent and different lines from Nicolay and Hay, had also published a biography. His Lincoln was different from the one whom they had known; theirs was the President, his the small-town lawyer and politician. Their intimate acquaintance with Lincoln began about the time his ended. Their interest lay in Lincoln's achievements, Herndon's in his ancestry and pre-presidential years, in an analysis and explanation of his characteristics. Thus his work and theirs were complementary.

Herndon began to collect material soon after Lincoln became President, although at that time he had no definite idea of writing a book. After Lincoln's death he visited the Kentucky, Indiana, and Illinois neighborhoods where Lincoln had lived, and interviewed and corresponded with people who had known him. In the course of his investigations he visited New Salem. He knew something of the village at first hand, for his father had owned land in that vicinity, and he had visited his cousins, James and Rowan Herndon, when they lived there. He had followed the *Talisman* up the Sangamon, and had known Lincoln as early as 1834. From 1847 to 1860 he handled his and Lincoln's legal business in Menard County.

As Herndon interviewed old settlers they groped back through the intervening years, recalling New Salem incidents and personalities. He found their recollections vivid, for, as he said: "Lincoln had great individuality which he never sank in the mob. His individualism stood out from the mass of men like a lone cliff over the plains below." By patient and persistent work Herndon accumulated a mass of testimony. He used part of his material in a series of lectures and sold copies of some of it to Ward Hill Lamon, who used it in a biography of Lincoln that was published in 1872. Herndon's book appeared in 1889.

Herndon was largely responsible for arousing popular interest in Lincoln's early life and environment, yet he failed to appreciate or fully understand the influence of that environment. He, like Nicolay and Hay, regarded it almost wholly as a handicap. He conceived of Lincoln as rising from "a stagnant, putrid pool" and contrasted his early life and background with his accomplishments.

Ida M. Tarbell was the first to see Lincoln's frontier surroundings as an energizing and constructive force. She began her research shortly after Herndon's book appeared, when, acting upon the suggestion of the editors of *McClure's Magazine*, she set out to interview those acquaintances of Lincoln's who were still alive, to study Lincoln's ancestry, and visit and photograph places associated with him and his progenitors. She began to realize the vigor, the independence, the democracy of the frontier, to see that, while pioneer life

was often poor and hard, it was not sordid, hopeless, or
belittling. Miss Tarbell, like Herndon, did much to
create interest in Lincoln's background and development, yet after intensive study of both his heredity and

THE INTERIOR OF HENRY ONSTOT'S HOUSE

environment, in her earlier books she saw him primarily
as "the flowering of generations of upright, honorable
men."

Perhaps a fuller understanding of the frontier influence on Lincoln was not possible without a clearer
realization of the part the frontier played in shaping

American institutions and ideals. At any rate, it was only after the development of the "frontier hypothesis" by Frederick Jackson Turner and his school of historians that writers began to see Lincoln's early environment in something like its true perspective, to realize that, while it was raw and crude in many ways and imposed seeming hardships and difficulties, yet it was what had nurtured him; that he succeeded not in spite of, but— in some respects, at least—because of it. Miss Tarbell in her later books, and especially in *In the Footsteps of the Lincolns,* published in 1924, gave Lincoln's surroundings and associates a more prominent place as factors in his development. Louis A. Warren devoted a large portion of his *Lincoln's Parentage and Childhood* to Lincoln's Kentucky environment and its influence. Carl Sandburg in the preface to his *Abraham Lincoln: The Prairie Years* noted that Lincoln was "keenly sensitive to the words and ways of people around him. Therefore those people, their homes, occupations, songs, proverbs, schools, churches, politics, should be set forth with the incessant suggestion of change that went always with pioneer life. They are the backgrounds on which the life of Lincoln moved, had its rise and flow, and was moulder and moulded."

As this conception gained gradual acceptance, people in increasing numbers began to visit Hodgenville, the place of Lincoln's birth, and to follow the route the Lincolns trod in their migration from Kentucky through Indiana to Illinois, visiting the places associated with his life, trying to visualize his surroundings. There was growing demand for the marking of the route and the restoration of the more important places. In 1887 Robert Lincoln presented the Lincoln home in Springfield to the State of Illinois. Later the state acquired the old capitol at Vandalia where Lincoln sat as a legislator, the courthouse at Metamora where he practiced law, and the Coles County farm of his parents. The Lincoln Centennial in 1909 did much to promote the preservation of local traditions and create wider interest in the general Lincoln story. From 1906 to 1911, 81,000 people enrolled in the Lincoln Farm Association and contributed amounts from twenty-five cents to twenty-five dollars for the purchase of the Lincoln birthplace farm and cabin and the erection of a memorial there. The memorial was dedicated in 1916 and turned over to the Federal government. In 1922 the Lincoln Circuit-Marking Association, formed under the auspices of the Illinois Chapter of the Daughters of the American Revolution, undertook to mark the route followed by Lincoln when he practiced law on the Eighth Judicial Circuit. In 1929 the Abraham Lincoln Association stated one of its purposes to be "to preserve and make more readily accessible the landmarks associated with his life." The states of Kentucky, Indiana, and

Illinois undertook to ascertain and mark the route of the Lincoln migration. Interest in Lincoln's background and development eventually eclipsed the interest in his achievements as a president.

In so far as New Salem was concerned, the realization came that Lincoln did not dominate the place, but was both in and of it; that, while he influenced its life, more important was the mark it left on him. William E. Barton, writing in 1925, called New Salem "Lincoln's Alma Mater."

With the growth of the Lincoln legend in Menard County came the belief that New Salem had not yet fulfilled its destiny. In 1902 T. G. Onstot in his *Pioneers of Menard and Mason Counties* asserted that it was destined to become the "Mount Vernon of the West." Onstot wrote his book at the insistence of old settlers who wished to keep alive the story of the community. The Old Salem Chautauqua, organized in 1897, held its meetings across the river from the deserted village and helped perpetuate its memory. In 1906 William Randolph Hearst delivered a lecture before this association and afterward was taken to the site of New Salem. His interest was aroused to such an extent that he purchased a sixty-two-acre tract containing the site for $11,000 and conveyed it to the Chautauqua Association in trust.

In January 1917 the people of Petersburg organized the Old Salem Lincoln League, with fifty charter members. July 4, 1917, the League held a picnic at New Salem and invited all old settlers who had knowledge of the town to attend this gathering. With the help of these old people the sites of several cabins were located and the old roads were traced and marked. On January 4, 1918, the League was incorporated and began a drive for funds with which to continue the work of restoration. Under its auspices, and as Menard County's part in the celebration of the Illinois Centennial in 1918, a pageant depicting episodes in Lincoln's life was given at New Salem. Log cabins were erected on the sites of the Rutledge tavern, the Lincoln-Berry store, the Offutt store, the Hill-MacNamar store, and Dr. Allen's residence. These were not authentic reproductions, and were subsequently torn down. In addition, the League published a book, *Lincoln at New Salem,* by Thomas P. Reep, thereby putting into permanent form the mass of information it had gathered about the village and the families that had lived there.

The pageant and the book stirred interest far and wide and did much to make New Salem a place of pilgrimage. The idea of restoring the village was enthusiastically accepted, and on April 3, 1919, the Illinois Legislature, acceding to the public desire, agreed to take over the sixty-two-acre tract, maintain it as a state park, and eventually restore all buildings that were there in Lincoln's time. With Mr. Hearst's consent the Old Salem Chautauqua Association deeded the land to the state, which erected a museum and purchased an additional twenty-acre tract adjoining Mr. Hearst's purchase.

In 1932 the work of restoration was begun. It was preceded by intensive research. Every available bit of information about New Salem was collected and collated. Lincoln biographies, contemporary letters, public records, and reminiscences of New Salem residents and their descendants yielded useful information. The investigations made by the Old Salem Lincoln League were of inestimable value.

The first problem was to locate the various cabin sites. The original plat of New Salem, on file in the Recorder's Office, gave the numbers and dimensions of the lots, the width of Main Street (sixty feet), and its compass direction, but did not locate the town with respect to section lines. By studying the available records of surveys made in connection with land transfers in New Salem, however, and by making some necessary corrections in them, the surveyors were able to locate the north and south lot lines. The east and west lot lines were located—with the possibility of a slight variation—by means of the old basements.

The lots having been relocated, the sites of most of the cabins could be identified. The site of Dr. Allen's residence was located for the Old Salem Lincoln League in 1918 by Mrs. Louisa Clary, who lived in New Salem about 1840; and her identification is confirmed by a deed showing conveyance of this lot to Allen. Mrs. Clary also pointed out the locations of Hill's residence and store and the Lincoln-Berry store. Her identification of the two former places is also confirmed by a deed showing title in Hill. Clary's grocery and Offutt's store had been located years before by old settlers, and the remaining houses were located either by deeds or by discovery of the old basements. When deeds were lacking, identification was made by means of maps, or, rather, crude drawings of the village. Six of these are in existence, and, while they all contain errors and inconsistencies and are not drawn to scale, they give an idea of the positions of the various cabins with respect to one another.[1]

In many instances excavation of the old cellars uncovered the piers of the original foundations, with the old lime mortar clinging to the stones. The ruins of an outside cellar were found near the site of the Rutledge tavern. The exact dimensions of most of the cellars could be ascertained by noting the difference in color between the newly spaded virgin soil and the filled-in earth. Frequently the number of rooms in a cabin was

[1] They were drawn respectively by W. H. Herndon, Mrs. Samuel Hill, T. G. Onstot, R. J. Onstot, J. McCan Davis, and Henry C. Whitney.

determined by the size and shape of the excavation. In two or three cases indications of an outside cellar door were detected.

Discovery of pieces of broken brick, mortar, and ashes revealed the position of most of the fireplaces; and this in turn showed the direction of the ridgepoles, for the chimney was invariably built at one of the gable ends of the house because of the added support obtained there. The New Salem settlers found stone for fireplaces, chimneys, and foundations, and excellent clay for bricks close by. The bricks used in the restored houses are the same kind found in the excavations, and are made of clay from a pit just southwest of New Salem hill.

In general, the New Salem cabins were superior to those built in Indiana and southern Illinois; for by the time the pioneers reached central Illinois many of them had had previous experience in cabin-building. The first cabins in New Salem were of simple construction, but with the completion of the mill, the coming of the blacksmith and other mechanics, and the opening of contacts with Cincinnati, New Orleans, and St. Louis, better workmanship and materials were available, and more comfortable houses were built.

In order to work out the details of the cabins it was necessary to collect all available data regarding their occupants. The date of a man's arrival, the number of

children he had, his occupation, the part he played in
village activities all gave clues as to the type of house
he lived in. Dr. Allen, for example, was well educated, a
good businessman, and accustomed to comfortable living. Consequently, his house is one of the better ones.
The fireplace and chimney have been built of stone
because Allen could afford that type of construction.
The house sometimes served as a church and school and
general meeting-place, so the opening between the living-
room and one of the bedrooms has been left wide on the
assumption that it was hung with portieres that could
be pushed back to allow both rooms to be used when
people gathered there.

Since Samuel Hill was married on July 28, 1835,
it was presumed that his house was built sometime between April and July of that year. By that date the
mill was in operation, the blacksmith was in town, and
good materials could be had. Hill was a prosperous
man, and his wife was a woman of good taste. Hence
their residence is the finest in town, the only one with
two stories and a porch. It has doors front and rear, an
outside cellar entrance, and a sliding window such as
was used only in the more pretentious homes.

Peter Lukins was a shoemaker, and a shop room
has been added to his house. Since his cabin was one of
the earlier ones, it has been simply built, with notched
corners, puncheon floor, wood mantel, and "cat and

clay" chimney. Robert Johnson, the wheelwright, must also have had a workshop in connection with his house. Johnson was a man of moderate means, so his house is unpretentious. The floor is made of puncheons, and latches, hinges, and other fittings are of wood. The original iron kettle used by Martin Waddell, the hatter, has been preserved. It is too large to have sat in a fireplace, and must have been used out of doors. Consequently, a porch roof has been built on the east side of Waddell's house, where he would have been least exposed as he worked, and the kettle now hangs there. Since Waddell was not well-to-do, his house has a puncheon floor and wooden hinges and locks. Windows are small and fixed in place.

Joshua Miller and John Kelso married sisters, and their house was double—really two houses with an opening between and a continuous roof and floor. This type of cabin was popular in the West and is often seen in the South today. It was assumed that the Kelsos, being childless, lived in one room, while the Millers, who had two children, had two rooms. Since Miller was a blacksmith, one of the windows in his cabin is an ingenious sliding type similar to the one in Hill's house, and all fittings are of iron.

Barrels were in great demand in the New Salem community, and Henry Onstot, the cooper, was a prosperous man. Moreover, his house was built in 1835,

when good workmanship and materials were available.
Hence it has stone fireplaces, chimneys, and mantels,
brick hearths, floor of sawn boards, and iron locks,
latches, and hinges. Clary's grocery, on the other hand,

ROBERT JOHNSON'S SHOP

was one of the first structures to be built and was purely
utilitarian in character. It has only one room, with fireplace and chimney made of logs and plastered sticks,
and a wooden mantel. Floors, windows, doors, and log
corners are of relatively crude construction. The roof

is built of clapboards or shingles, held in place by log "weight poles," instead of nails.

The carding-machine, one of the most interesting structures in the village, with its huge treadmill on which a yoke of oxen plodded stolidly at their work, is equipped with a double carder, typical of the period, that was built by Schofield Brothers in Massachusetts in 1804 from patterns smuggled into the United States from England. Four oxen, stabled in Hill's barn, though never used on the treadmill, often draw a covered wagon through the village streets.

In 1940 the U. S. Postmaster General, in acknowledgment of Lincoln's service as a postmaster, decided to reopen the New Salem post office. It is located in the first Lincoln-Berry store, which they bought from the Herndon brothers. Though this structure never served as a post office during the life of the village, it was considered the most practical place for present-day postal service.

Besides necessitating a thorough study of the village and its inhabitants, the reconstruction presented technical problems. Walls had to be built in some cellars where they did not exist because of the danger of cave-ins. Stone foundations had to be built down below the frost line, although the originals did not go that deep. Since the logs could not be painted, they were treated with zinc chloride to make them impervious to insects and decay. Warping of puncheon floors had to be guarded against. A type of plaster that would be more durable than the mixture of lime mortar or mud and hair used by the pioneers, but would have the same appearance, had to be devised. Cement, mixed with hair and colored to resemble mud, was used. The terrain of New Salem hill has changed in one hundred years. The ravine east of the Lincoln-Berry store, for example, had cut back many feet, and an extensive fill was necessary to restore the former topography.

When the state took over the task of reconstruction the Old Salem Lincoln League devoted itself to securing furnishings for the cabins. Within a relatively short time it had collected over 900 articles. Most of these were contributed by descendants of pioneer settlers of Menard County. Every piece was passed on by an authenticity committee, and unless an article was obviously one hundred years old the donors were required to trace its history back a hundred years before it was accepted. The people of Menard County and some from more distant places were most generous in turning over old pieces of furniture and relics to the state. Not a single piece was bought.[2]

A few of the articles were actually used at New

[2] The State of Illinois has published a *Catalogue of New Salem Collection of Pioneer Relics,* prepared by the New Salem Lincoln League. This gives a description and history of each article of furniture.

Salem. Among these are a spindle-back, wood-bottom chair used in the Rutledge tavern while Onstot was proprietor; a trunk, brought from Ohio by Dr. Regnier in 1828; two wooden benches from Dr. Regnier's office; a sewing-basket owned by Mrs. Hill; a whisky flask and dish purchased at the Offutt store. In the Hill residence are two blanket chests owned by Mrs. Hill and brought from Kentucky by her family, a handmade wooden foot-stool, a chest of drawers, two hickory-bottom chairs, a hammer, and two plates, all owned by Mrs. Hill, and a trunk and handmade gun hooks owned by Samuel Hill. On the bottom of the trunk is written: "McNeal & Hill, St. Louis, Missouri." From various parts of the country descendants of New Salem residents sent these relics back to adorn the reconstructed cabins of their former owners.

All the articles are reminiscent of pioneer days and give a picture of the life and origin of the community— a cotton gin made at Rock Creek; a Boston rocker brought from New York state to Athens, Illinois, in 1818; a chair in which Eliza Church, holding her baby in her arms, sat in a covered wagon during the ride from Massachusetts to Illinois sometime in the twenties; a pewter "sugar and creamer" brought to Illinois in a covered wagon in the thirties; a platter owned by Frances Green Armstrong, sister-in-law of Jack Armstrong; a sideboard brought from Kentucky in a covered wagon; a long-neck, clear-blown glass bottle given to the Clary's Grove Baptist Church for use in the communion service.

The residence of Peter Lukins is equipped with furniture from the house of Charles James Fox Clarke, erected near New Salem in 1839. At one time Clarke was a cobbler and cabinetmaker, and most of this furniture was made by him. It had never been moved from the old home until placed in Lukins's cabin.

In 1953 an impressive nine-foot bronze statue depicting Lincoln as he left New Salem for a larger life was commissioned for the entrance to the village. The work of the celebrated sculptor, Avard Fairbanks, it is a gift of the Sons of Utah Pioneers to the State of Illinois.

And so New Salem stands again. And in imagination we can see Onstot, Waddell, Ferguson, busy at their work, Kelso strolling toward the river with his fishing-pole, Hill behind his counter, Miller at his forge, Allen visiting the sick. We can hear the creaking of the carding-machine, listen to the gossip in the stores, and watch a horse race or a wrestling-match. We can see the people turning out to vote, riding into town on Saturday to stock up with supplies and have their "fling," greeting the stage as it pulls up the steep hill.

We can picture Lincoln coming here at twenty-two, an unknown, unschooled youth—clerking in the store, joining the boys in their rough-and-tumble sports, rapidly establishing himself. We can see him talking, joking, arguing theology, discussing politics, learning to know these people, winning their confidence. We see him studying, developing, rising from laborer to postmaster, surveyor, legislator. We see him when he leaves at twenty-eight and realize that he has found himself.

And implanted deep within him, as he silently rode away, was a conviction of the essential worth and right-mindedness of ordinary people. Born largely of the kindness and helpfulness he had known at New Salem, it was a faith that would one day prove momentous for men the whole world over.

INDEX